Careful Where You Set This Down

A Strategic Guide to Heal the Hoarder in You

by
Angel Peterson

JOURNEY SERIES
Angel Peterson Publishing

Copyright © 2016
Angel Peterson, All Rights Reserved.

All rights reserved. No part of this book may be reproduced or transmitted in any form or by any means, electronic or mechanical, including photocopying, recording or by any information storage and retrieval system, without written permission from the author, except for the inclusion of brief quotations in a review.

Published by:
Angel Peterson Publishing
Calgary, Alberta   CANADA

Peterson, Angel C.D., 1975, Author
CAREFUL WHERE YOU SET THIS DOWN
A Strategic Guide to Healing the Hoarder in You

Angel C.D. Peterson

Published in Canada

First Angel Peterson printing: November 2016
10 9 8 7 6 5 4 3 2 1
ISBN: 978-0-9950780-0-0

All information in this book is based on personal experience. It is sold with the understanding that the author and publisher are not engaged in rendering legal, clinical, psychological, or otherwise professional advice.

The author and publisher specifically disclaim any liability that is incurred from the use or application of the contents of this book.

If you do not wish to be bound by the above, you may return this book to the publisher for a refund.

FOR:

My children... my WHY!

You four are the reason I stayed the course and didn't give up on myself.

Also for my mom

You gave me a beautiful example of what I could be.

"The belongings people accumulate throughout their lives will always own them. People seem to think if they had more they'd be happier or freer, but their possessions only chain them to the earth."

- Sarah Noffke, Awoken

TABLE OF CONTENTS

Acknowledgements 1

Introduction 3

Part I: INSIGHT 5

    Chapter 1: The Beginning 7

    Chapter 2: Road Blocks and Recovery 13

Part II: LEARN FROM MY JOURNEY 33

    Chapter 3: The Start: Creating a Beautiful Space 35

    Chapter 4: Wiping Out the Cancerous Clutter 40

    Chapter 5: A Look Inside 44

    Chapter 6: Stumbles Backslides and Getting Back Up 51

    Chapter 7: Major Blows 56

    Chapter 8: Growing Through Grief 61

    Chapter 9: Picking up the Pieces 67

    Chapter 10: Putting My Foot Down on Excuses 74

    Chapter 11: Growth... Six Years Later 81

    Chapter 12: Love and Forgiveness 88

    Chapter 13: 2016 Progress Setbacks and Insights 97

    Chapter 14: Patterns and Shame 103

    Chapter 15: It's All Perspective 110

    Chapter 16: Defining Ownership 118

Chapter 17: A Look Into the Past 122

Chapter 18: Onward! 130

Chapter 19: Scars and Healing 136

Chapter 20: Discovery 142

Chapter 21: Flashback to the Start 151

Part III: REFLECTION 163

Chapter 22: Fishing for Meaning 165

Part IV: DO 171

Chapter 23: The Transformation 173

Chapter 24: Advanced Advice 202

Helpful Music Playlist 213

Daily Intentions and Action Steps 215

Space Creation Affirmations Tear Out Page 217

ACKNOWLEDGEMENTS

- Mom, for helping me through the years, never giving up on me even when I had, and for showing me that I am worth more.

- My children for being my light through all our darkness, for forgiving me all we've been through together and for loving me unconditionally as I love them.

- My father who always believed in me.

- Barbara Ellison for her dream coaching and our wonderful talks that led to some powerful breakthroughs.

- My friend Tamia Dow for providing feedback and the great idea to add journaling throughout the book.

- Brigitta Hoeferle, my life coach who kept me on track and gave me encouragement to continue on and helped me celebrate each success no matter its size.

- Jennifer Low for her encouragement.

- Blanka Boschnak for our wonderful talks and mutual help throughout our journeys.

- Jamie Lehr for reading and giving me feedback and for your excitement.

- Heidy Panameno for being such a wonderful friend who has accepted me at my worst and my best.

- Terri Lynn Hayman who helped me in the past and was always like an older sister to me, though so much younger.

- Curtis LaBelle who was a great friend when I most needed one.

- The Global Mastermind Program family who have always filled me with encouragement and helpful information on improving myself and my business.

- Michael Silvers who gave me direction.
- Tina Colbert from Balboa Press, division of Hay House who called me and got the ball rolling again. I wouldn't have picked this up and finished it before our deadline had we not talked.
- New Peaks and the many wonderful volunteers who helped me on my journey the last couple of years by helping me believe in me to know that I have what it takes to do whatever I dream of. You all reminded me of my dad who always told me I could do whatever I put my mind to.
- All of my numerous teachers throughout my life, intentional and unintentional. The good, the bad and the ugly. You were all a part of the process.
- Sharon Jensen, my Editor, who helped me make my book pretty, have a little better flow, and get the finished product to press.

INTRODUCTION

I found it very interesting reading this script 5 years after I had first written it to see how the clutter had spilled over into all areas of my life... even into the words I had written.

My writing was cluttered. There is often no clear meaning in my attempt to introduce order with my dates and topic headings before I edited.

I made the process of reading more difficult than it needed to be with a plethora of words used where one would do.

This book was written by me as advice to myself. If it helps you, either to understand a hoarder, or to heal your own hoarder inside, that will have made coming out of the overstuffed closet to share this shameful side of my past all worthwhile.

Part I

Insight

Chapter 1
THE BEGINNING

I remember back to when I was a cute little pig-tailed girl old enough to be in a store alone; young enough to still feel excited by it. Mom brought my brother and me to the arcade while she shopped for groceries. She gave each of us a quarter to spend on whichever game we chose. My brother headed straight to his favourite game with a big smile across his face. I stood by him and watch him play until his game was over and a frown replaced the smile.

It felt like such a waste to me to play for a couple of minutes or less and then the quarter is gone. I walked to each game and stood in front of it long enough to get a feel for its purpose and then moved on to the next.

This was the routine each shopping trip with mom. Each trip, I decided this was the day I would pick a game and play it. Each day, mom would arrive before my quarter was spent.

My brother eventually began begging me for my unspent quarters for another chance to win his at favourite game since I wasn't going to spend it anyways. The decision was so difficult for me... I couldn't choose between them all.

I always had such a hard time making decisions... and not just with video games. I'd often stand in front of a fast food menu until the people in line behind me would start shuffling around impatiently or mom would give me the ultimatum to, "pick something now or go without."

Dad used to say I was great at saving money but if I had more of it, I'd have just picked everything. The choice to pick one meant saying no to all the rest and the longer I stalled, the longer all of the possibilities were open to me. So I didn't choose.

On the occasions when I was forced to pick something from the menu when dining out and everyone's food had arrived, I found myself no longer wanting what I had; instead I wanted what everyone else had.

So making the choice was the wrong choice for me. Instead of picking and having one and not all the rest, I ended up with none, and I was more okay with that than if I had made the choice.

The arcade quarters started to grow and eventually I bought a box of chocolate mints with it, ate one or two, and hid the rest in a shoebox under my bed. This was my special stash. I was proud of my ability to save because it meant I got to have treats... until one day when I went to retrieve my mints and there were none to be found. I assumed the mint raider was my brother and that I couldn't trust the shoebox to protect my treasures any longer.

I don't know if this contributed to my problems, but it does give insight into how my mind worked. I still don't like making choices. If I don't make a strong intention to the contrary, I'll purchase all instead of narrowing down to the best. This is whether it's food, clothing, books, toys or anything else.

No wonder the kids prefer Christmas with me. I have such difficulty putting things back from my cart or choosing between many great options, so they tend to get spoiled.

May 19, 2010

Hoarding isn't about being lazy. I thought it was for the longest time and I know others think that as well. This is so much more complicated than laziness. Something that should be a simple job like putting away groceries, becomes a project that could take hours, days, or never, depending on the state of the house and the mind.

If there is space and the fridge is clean then it's no problem. But, add on the issues of having to make space in the fridge for the new groceries, having to clean the fridge first, sorting through rotten food to make room to get it cleaned, having a place to set the groceries down while making space in and cleaning the fridge first, needing to clear out the sink for the hot soapy water or finding a bucket and room to set the bucket down near to the fridge so the molded rotten smelly spills can be cleaned up.

Then add on having to find a clean rag and some detergent in order to clean up those spills before putting away the nice, fresh, beautiful new groceries, being able to get to the fridge without tripping on everything on the floor, being able to open the front door to the house wide enough to allow both you and the grocery bags inside. You get the picture... it is not a pretty one.

So once again you have given up before you even fully get through the front door. The nice meal you had visualized and planned out at the grocery store becomes overshadowed by overwhelm.

You then drop the bags inside the front door or on whatever space there is, or make room by shoving stuff over with your foot, grab the handy oversized bag of potato chips instead and, after you push the clean laundry pile in need of folding over far enough to allow you bum space, you plop down on the couch to watch TV... but you can't find the remote in the mess so you just watch whatever channel it was last stuck on; either news or Hannah Montana.

After a while you might try to shove the frozen food into the freezer or perishables into the fridge... over, under, and sideways just to get it to stay, then pray it doesn't all come toppling out the next time the fridge door is opened.

Hopefully nothing is left in the bags that will rot right away because it could be a few days (if ever) before those groceries get properly put away. At least they are close to the TV for snacking on when hunger strikes. Then with a fridge that is too full, nothing can be found, just like in the house, so the food that is there gets wasted when it rots behind the new purchases.

It is overwhelming. So...how do we get to the space where we can actually shop for groceries, come home, put the food away, and prepare the nice meal we had envisioned and sit down at the dinner table together as a family to eat without tripping on the way?

It won't happen overnight, and if it does, if you are a hoarder/cluttered living person, then it is only a temporary solution.

I've been there many times before. I want this to become my past. I don't want it around forever or even another year. If this were a person, I would not want to marry it or even invite it over for a while, but this relationship has lasted longer than most marriages including my own and has been the plague that led to the death of many more.

This isn't something that I want in my life any longer, and it won't go away without changing how I do things, and how I see things.

I really hope that my experiences can help others recover as well.

Take a moment to commit to your healing.

Decide how much longer you want to have this relationship instead of enriching the relationship with other people, or even with yourself.

I _____ commit to the process of healing. I reject hoarding and that which does not serve me. Instead I embrace a life filled with wonderful possibilities, healthy relationships, and a healthy mind and home.

Date: _____

Signature: _____

Chapter 2

ROAD BLOCKS AND RECOVERY

What keeps us from "cleaning up our act"? Generally these will fall into one of two main categories: physical and emotional. Distractions could be a possible subcategory to the emotional category.

PHYSICAL

Lack of Organization

Without a designated place to put things, so much time is wasted. This can lead to many other road blocks. For instance; if you don't have one place (and only one) to put your car keys, you'll be late for everything.

You'll spend 10-30 minutes of every morning before you leave your house in a panic, and likely you'll make a heck of a mess looking for them... that is no way to start your morning.

Have you ever tried turning around a day that's gone all wrong from the start? Not so easy. You can't find things when you don't have a place for them and this often leads to buying doubles and more of what you already have. This is a waste of money, time, and space.

Soon you will be unable to keep anything clean because you will have too much stuff for the space you have. You will have unnecessarily spent money that could be used for something more enjoyable that would not add to your clutter and would enrich your lives, like a trip or a class to learn something that would benefit your life.

You want to give yourself every chance at success and happiness. Organization doesn't have to be a dirty word and just because you aren't naturally organized, it doesn't mean you can never become organized. It can be learned.

Too Much Stuff, Not Enough Space

I moved from a gorgeous new 2300 square foot house with 4600 sq. ft. of finished living space including the basement to a 30+ year old 900 sq. ft. falling-apart trailer.

That was painful for more than the obvious reasons. I had stuff stacked outside of my house for months that I just could not fit inside and could not bear to throw out or give away. Nobody wanted to buy it either.

Even once those things were gone, after I'd eventually gotten rid of them *(which felt so painful while it happened, but not so painful now... and now five years later, freeing and peaceful without it all, like the shackles and chains were removed and buried)*, I would go shopping at second hand stores or garage sales and come home with my arms packed full of "deals" and no place to put them.

Then I would wonder why it was so much easier to get the house clean when we first moved in and so difficult to clean it now.

Multiples of an Item

When I couldn't find something I needed, I would buy another. I had three whisks, two can openers, four rolling pins (and I hadn't even used one of them in 7 years) and many other doubles, triples, and more of things that I only needed one of. I actually caught myself more than once buying another of something I had just bought the week before because it was a better deal than the original one I had bought.

Yes I am just as aware of how crazy that is as you are, but it didn't stop me from doing it. This is a sickness, or a mental blockage or something else I haven't fully figured out yet. These stories sound funny, I know, but they are also sad.

Write down some of your own habits and actions that you have become aware of that make sense to you at the time, but wouldn't make sense if you start to explain it to someone. This is to make you aware of your actions... not to change them yet, but just to be conscious of your own thought processes and actions.

_____
_____
_____
_____
_____
_____
_____
_____
_____
_____

Drowning in Laundry and Dishes

Make sure that you don't have more clothes than will fit in your closet and drawers when they are all cleaned. If you have clothes that your children have outgrown, get rid of them, sell them, give them away to charity or throw them out.

I know it is hard to get rid of them when you've spent so much money on them or if it was made for your child or it was just really cute, but this is the type of thing that if held on to, will detract from your life. The type of thing you have to ask yourself is "Do I want to keep this, or do I want to enrich the relationship with the person it reminds me of?"

Take a moment to ask yourself this question and write down what comes up for you.

_____
_____
_____
_____
_____
_____
_____
_____
_____
_____
_____
_____
_____

Unfinished Tasks

Prior to editing, my cluttered mind had named this "Unfinished Partially Completed Tasks Undone" *(or as I've edited 5 years later "Unfinished Tasks").* When tasks are incomplete, you often need to start all over. This happens when you do the work, and then do it again and again without ever fully completing the job. In laundry, it's when you wash your clothes, even fold them nicely but you don't put them away.

Then they get scattered on the floor, trampled on, dirtied again or dirty clothes get taken off and thrown down on top of the clean ones, which happens when piles of folded laundry get placed in the rooms they belong in but not put away into drawers, due to already overcrowded drawers or simply not finishing the job fully, thus creating a new need for laundering.

This same thing could happen with dishes, or a nice big meal fully prepared and only partially eaten. If it is not put away into containers in the fridge, it will go bad. Dirty dishes left to sit will take so much more time and effort to clean than dishes washed right away.

A floor swept up without the pile put in a dustpan and then into the trash can easily be stepped through and spread all around causing the need to sweep again. Instead, complete all steps then put the trash outside in a canister every day so that it doesn't smell up the house and pets don't have the chance to get into it and spread it all around.

All of these instances make more work for you than there should be. You don't want to have to do the job more than once. Even twice is too much. Make the first time count by fully completing the task so that you don't sabotage yourself into having to do it all over again. It is exhausting. You should only have to clean up one home.

If you aren't completing the jobs, it is as if you are cleaning up 3 or 4 or more homes depending on how long you let it go on for. My mom used to think I was lying when she'd call me daily and ask what I was doing... I would answer "cleaning", yet my house stayed horrible. This is why this seemingly conundrum-like riddle can be true. I thought it was strange too that every time she'd call me, I would be cleaning yet getting no cleaner.

Think about how long you would take to finish the tasks completely compared to how much time you spend to redo the task multiple times.

_____
_____
_____
_____
_____
_____

What are some of the tasks you often leave unfinished?

_____
_____
_____
_____
_____
_____
_____
_____
_____

TIPS BROKEN DOWN FOR EASY APPLICATION

<u>Physical</u>

1. The old adage... a place for everything, and everything in its place.
2. Only keep what fits into your square footage.
3. Get rid of multiples (unless it's two adults in the bedroom, there's no need for multiples of anything).
4. Pare down laundry and dishes to what fits in the closet and cupboards comfortably. Get rid of what no longer serves you.
5. Complete tasks. Even if you don't finish the entire job, finish all the steps of the part you have done. For example: do one load of laundry from start to finish... from hamper to washer to dryer to folding to dresser.

"I am a rock, I am an island.

And a rock feels no pain,

and an island never cries"

~ **Simon and Garfunkel**

EMOTIONAL

It Feels Safe

I keep my house a disaster for the same reason I am overweight, because it makes me feel safer (at the time I wrote this, it was accurate, however now I want to change it to: I kept my house a disaster for the same reason I was overweight, it made me feel safer. This is no longer the case).

I am fat because I fear being hurt by another failed relationship or worse, a harmful relationship. I thought that having this extra weight would deter and lessen the romantic interest from men in a passive way. I wouldn't have to say no when the interest isn't there. With no interest, there is no relationship and therefore, no chance of being hurt by a man.

With my house, I don't have to let anyone inside when it is a mess, just like I don't have to let anyone inside my heart when I'm a mess. It is my protective shield. It is my wall.

Also somehow I rationalized that it would be safer inside of a messy house because if someone broke in, they couldn't move around without making noise, so I would know if there was an intruder.

I also thought that if anyone saw the inside of my house, they wouldn't want to put the effort into finding anything of monetary value or they would think that I have nothing of value judging from the state things are in... and maybe they would be right.

Write down some of the perceived benefits to having your home the state that it is in. This will help show you the areas you will be working on later and make you aware of why you turned to hoarding as a solution so that you can face those issues when you are ready.

_____

_____

_____

_____

_____

_____

_____

_____

_____

_____

_____

Precious Memories

My stuff holds precious memories of a time when things were better. Though I like change in my life, and even crave it, I don't like to see things change. I love nostalgia.

When I see a toy that I grew up with in a second hand store, it makes me feel good. Usually I buy the toy thinking my kids might like it. They almost never do, but more than that, it usually can't be found again to be played with or it gets broken because it doesn't have a home, so it is put in a pile which gets stepped on eventually.

The feeling that I felt in the store looking at the toy gets replaced by frustration once I get it home... when it gets broken, once it adds to my clutter and mess, and when I realize all the money I've spent on these items that never get used or get broken before they have the chance to be used. It is not worth it to own anymore.

I hate when things get changed or get updated. I wish I could go back into my old elementary school and see exactly what I left behind. I wish I could go to my old park and swing on the same swings. I wish I could play on the same dirt hill and climb the same tree in the field that is now a neighbourhood, but things change. I guess they have to.

I am a nostalgic person rather than nouveau. It isn't unusual for me to have dreams about my old bedroom and all of my old toys or even a coin I'd lost. I still remember losing two dollars when I was about 9. I felt bad about that for years. My mind doesn't let go of things.

Again, when I wrote this, it was accurate. Now I give myself permission to let go of things. It is okay that I had an attachment back then because that is where I was in my life. Now I choose to let go and experience every moment and make beautiful memories... not so that I have them to live off of when times are bad, but because they happen naturally when fully living and enjoying life.

I also give myself permission to let go of those memories and to forget, if that happens, because I know that there will be more and more beautiful moments to come.

Ask yourself, "If I could choose to have only my past memories and no new experiences that would feel and be even better than those moments the memories came from... or none of the past memories knowing that my future will be filled with so many moments that are much more precious than my past memories, which would I choose? Why?

_____
_____
_____
_____
_____
_____
_____
_____

Does my answer make sense? Does that lead me to a happier life in the future or does it keep me in a low state? What might I want to change?

_____
_____
_____
_____
_____
_____
_____
_____
_____
_____

Waste

Waste feels wrong. I don't like it. Yet when I end up having four of something I need only one of, it is a waste. When I buy something that doesn't even get used once because it gets lost or broken before I have a chance to use it, it is waste.

I don't want to throw things out in case I need them later or if I can't find it when I need to use it (this is when I'd usually end up going out to buy that item again and adding to the multiples). That is the definition of irony.

FINANCIAL STRAIN

I feel that I don't have the money to be wasting by getting rid of the things I've spent good money on. It hurts me to get rid of something I've spent money on (even a small amount) because I end up beating myself up about it later when I am lacking financially.

Again it leads back to the waste. I hate to waste things. This is another reason I am overweight. I can't waste good food. I've eaten the food left on my kid's plates. I am not proud of this... though I am not proud of much of what I have shared in this book.

I have picked up food from the floor to eat when my floors were not clean. I've scraped off mold or tried to salvage food that should be thrown out because I hate for it to be wasted, yet it is more of a waste to eat when it winds up adding to my size or to my health risks I no longer do this. I think after I wrote it down and realized how awful it was, I didn't do it as often until eventually I just stopped... more irony yet again. Plus it is gross, but my mind learned to accept the disgusting when that's what it saw daily.

My lack led to more lack. The conundrum of feeling like I didn't have and wouldn't have enough led me to keeping everything, which led to more lack. It led to spending more money for all of the reasons I've already mentioned, which led to more financial strain.

If you were to live as though you will always have enough and that when you need something, you will be able to easily get it if you chose to and no one would be affected by your decision, would you change how you do things? Write down the thoughts that come up for you.

_____
_____
_____
_____
_____
_____
_____
_____
_____
_____
_____
_____
_____
_____

Overwhelm

In every sense of the word, being buried in clutter is overwhelming. The thought of getting organized seems impossible and I get tired just imagining the process. I usually quit before I ever start.

Sometimes it causes me to go out and shop for things I don't need because it feels better, or sometimes it causes me to go out and buy cleaning supplies because I think that if I bought them, I won't want to waste that money and it will motivate me into getting it done. Then that gets put on the kitchen table where I've cleared some space to get started, and it gets forgotten.

What are some of the ways you deal with your overwhelm?

_____
_____
_____
_____
_____
_____
_____
_____
_____

What are the ways you wish you would deal with it? You will get tips on dealing with overwhelm later in the book.

_____
_____
_____
_____
_____
_____
_____
_____
_____

LAUNDRY

Physical and Emotional

We have more clothes than we have space to put it. That means that it will always be a problem unless I get rid of the excess. What usually happens with laundry is, being in a household with three children, we get behind on laundry. Then when I do wash some loads, I almost never finish all of the laundry. The underwear and socks are often last so the kids tell me they have no socks or underwear.

It could be months before I actually find the socks and underwear to clean and months till I finally get fed up and get all of the laundry done, so I end up buying more.

I once bought close to $100 worth of socks because the kids needed them and we wanted to make sock monkeys for Christmas presents. We did manage to make the sweetest sock monkeys, but only a few.

Shortly after that the kids were asking for socks again...and I thought I wouldn't have to buy socks for a year.

I want to keep the clothes that my children outgrow for the next child, but there are 9 years between the youngest girl and her older sister. It is unlikely those clothes will even be found to be worn once she grows enough to fit them if I could even get her to wear them in another 7-9 years.

Of course the fond memories are attached to those clothes as well. How can I get rid of that dress that her grandmother made for her that still looks so adorable even with the black mold spots on the back of it from being left for days in the washer?

Well... I just threw it out without thinking about it, knowing it was now ruined and had to go. I took the plunge and chucked it in the trash, then took the trash outside so I wasn't tempted. I do not regret this. I may have regretted it back then. I do not regret it now.

SOLUTIONS AND TIPS

Emotional

1. **Safe / Self-Integrity.** When you learn to say no to what you don't want and are able to walk away from that which is harmful, then you begin to trust yourself and that wall becomes unnecessary.

2. **Memories.** Know that the memories of loved ones become clearer when your mind has less to sift through. Declutter your space, declutter your mind, and that will free up space to think more clearly and allow memories to come easier. Also get excited about the future. Your past isn't where you live anymore. Your future is open to being whatever you can imagine and work towards. Memories are nice to visit, but don't live there. If it helps you get to that point, take photos of what feels really important because of the memories attached to them.

3. **The Conundrum of Waste.** You'll be surprised to see how much richer you'll feel with the clutter gone. People pay money for space. Don't fill good space with waste. When you can find what you do have, you don't have to pay for it 3 times over or more and thus, you'll be saving money. Additionally, when you give your excess a new home, someone else gets to use what would be wasted, lost, or broken on your floors or in overflowing drawers or boxes where you can't find it.

4. **Changing Your Mindset from Scarcity to Abundance.** Purchase only what is needed and you'll find you have more money left. There is enough for everyone. When you feel you need another can of soup, go to the store and buy one... and only one, or at most enough for one or two meals until you are able to handle more than that without getting lost in too much once again.

   There is no need to have cupboards filled to overflowing just in case. Food expires, clothing goes out of fashion, too much piled up gets broken. What I get rid of can be bought for less than what it costs me emotionally to store it in my home, and often less than what it costs financially to store it in my home. Take care of what you do have after you've narrowed it down to a minimum, and you'll find that you have more than enough. It is very freeing.

5. **Make the Space... then the Overwhelm Disappears.** Think of it not that you are getting rid of valuable things, but that you are making or creating more space. Space is your most valuable possession.

6. **The Attachment to Clothing from Memories.** Better things are to come. When you can believe that, you'll start to see it, and then what you used to have becomes less important. Find importance instead in healthy relationships, knowledge and growth, experiences and moments that bring joy, and other similar type things that do not clutter your life but instead free your soul from the bondage of things. If you are not ready for that yet, you can take photos or bring the clothing to someone who will create a quilt from the fabric and have a comforting memory blanket made from the fabrics that brought so much comfort and lovely memories in the past.

I wouldn't suggest keeping it to make yourself because I know how those projects can add up and add to the stress, overwhelm, and clutter. You also can get rid of it and you will be alright.

Distractions

For myself, I had to get rid of my distractions in order to make a real difference to how I was living. The internet and television were ways that I could distract myself whenever I got too overwhelmed with my surroundings whether because of fighting unhappy kids, or the mess, bills, or everything that I needed to do but wanted to avoid.

If my kids started to fight while I was trying to clean, I'd give up and go on the computer. If I was bored or tired, I'd go on the computer. If I was lonely, I'd go on the computer or watch television. It is a crutch and a disease and I won't heal if I keep running away from life by diving into a life that isn't my own through the internet or television.

Even when I got so tired of being online and all the frustration that that world can bring, I still kept going back. I used to say I wanted to live my life instead of dream it away or have it all sucked away by being on the computer, but I wouldn't do anything about it. I really truly felt it, but without the action to change it, that feeling would never go away.

The morning before I started my great clean up, something just clicked in a now or never realization and I packed up the modem and cable box and drove off to Shaw Cable. They were so helpful in taking it back and cancelling my account. Maybe it helped that I had such resolve and a smile on my face. It almost felt like I'd been reborn that day with the sun shining and the birds chirping.

Maybe they always were singing away but I never noticed while I was preoccupied with the fantasy of online life, and I know I missed many blue skies cooped up at my desk in front of the computer screen. It is even hard now just sitting at the computer typing this out. The feeling I had while being online is similar to how this feels just sitting here typing. I'll have to be careful how I handle this.

The washer and dryer have been stopped for a while and I ignored it to keep typing just as I had in the past when I had internet. I should stop typing so that I can throw another load in and fold up the ones hot and fresh from the dryer before they lose that warmth (I could learn to love that feeling) and put them away before they fall, get walked on and dirty again before being worn. I don't know how many loads of clothes I've done and redone that hadn't had the chance to be worn simply because they got dirty again before they were put away.

Clothes rarely got put away before. This will be one of the tricks to getting and staying clean; to put away the clothes into drawers and hung up after they are fully dried so they don't get dirty again. I need to stop that awful and wasteful cycle.

I want to mention that the resolve to get rid of the distractions in my life had come and gone many times before. That is why I had to act on my impulse that moment without putting much thought into it before the moment had passed.

This is one of the tricks to changing. When the healthy impulses come, and they go against my usual habits and actions, I must act on them instantly before my bad habits and thoughts take over, thus keeping me from doing what is best for me.

The Solution

Fond memories have to be found in memories, not in stuff. I know it is sad to try to think back to a time and not be able to remember it clearly; but when you see something material from the past, it easily takes you back. Photos are wonderful for this, as are journals. I think more importantly; we are not done our lives. We should still be in the process of creating wonderful memories. If we aren't doing that now because our stuff is stealing that from us, we aren't living anymore. We aren't creating our lives; we are trying to relive what is already gone.

I don't want my things, my clutter, to steal my future. I don't want to hold on to THINGS anymore. I want to hold my children. I want to help my children to create fond memories and good habits. I don't want to pass my sickness on to my beautiful babies. As long as time is there to have, we aren't done living. By living in clutter, we allow that clutter to steal our precious time.

Cliché as it may be, **YOU ARE WORTH IT!** If this is a matter of keeping safe and keeping others out of my life, at what cost is it going to be? Trust isn't something I have to freely give away just because someone comes into my life. Trust should take time to build up.

Sometimes it is never earned. You don't have to let those people in that you don't trust. Even if you like them, you don't have to trust them. You can say no and must learn to say no in times when you feel a need to protect yourself or in times when you don't want to say yes. Practice saying no when you want to say no. Then stick to it. Clutter won't stop those bad things from happening. It won't stand in your defence. It will swallow you up if you allow it, and it is more harmful than the average person is to you.

Part II

THE journey

Chapter 3

CREATING A BEAUTIFUL SPACE

I share all of this to both keep track of my progress, and to write down the process in one place that I can come back to revisit later on and learn from, and also for you to take and adapt to your own life. Try on my system and see if it works for you and make adjustments where necessary. Remember; what I have done, you too can do.

If you would like more help with this, you can join my group coaching course, have one-on-one coaching or attend my "Slaying the Dragon" workshop.

May 15, 2010 – The Bedroom Sanctuary

I didn't try to get all the rooms cleaned by stuffing all the clutter into boxes, bins or bags like I would usually do. I ignored the clutter and mess for now, armed with my plan of action. I wanted one clean room... one safe place of relaxation. I thought the best place for that to be would be in my bedroom because it would do the most good for me in this huge undertaking. It would give me a place of refuge and renewal when I would need it the most in the midst of my mission.

My bedroom is usually the last place to get cleaned and the first place that all the boxes of homeless clutter get placed. The reason for cleaning my bedroom first this time is that my bedroom is the last place I see at night, and the first place I see in the morning.

How can the day have my best start when the first thing I see is mess? When I have to carefully make my way to the door past mounds of clean and dirty clothes and boxes and what not, then shove my door open into the mounds, pressing them together, just so I can exit my bedroom? How can I get a restful sleep when the last thing I see at night is chaos?

I decided to start with my bedroom, but first things first. My mom, who is an incredibly clean and organized beautiful lady and everything that I wish I was, always taught me that I should start every clean up with throwing a load of laundry in, then it works while I work. In the past this didn't always work for me because I forgot about many loads after they washed. They would sit for days all damp until they grew mildew and mold. I ruined many nice outfits this way. This time however, I was determined to remember, so I threw a load in and went to work on my bedroom.

When I needed a break from working on my bedroom, I either did laundry, or I started to prepare space to wash dishes. This took effort as there was no space on the counters and we actually started piling dirty pots and pans on the floor of our galley kitchen (our kitchen is dead centre of our trailer and is the only path to the bathroom). I accomplished space by nesting like things together. All the plates were stacked together, all the bowls together. The big things I put together on the floor so that I had space for drying dishes on the counter next to the sink.

Sometimes while doing the dishes, I closed my eyes and worked as if I were blind. Strangely this actually helped me as I could visualize a clean environment and not get overwhelmed so quickly. I had to be more cautious and it did slow me down, but it somehow energized me to keep going.

Once that got to be too much, I moved back into my bedroom to sort through five boxes of papers. It really felt like things were worse rather than better at first, but it's what I needed to do. I had a big garbage bag for obvious garbage and boxes for my sorting.

I felt so many emotions as I sorted through each piece of paper. Some made me smile. Those I often kept. Some made me downright mad and physically made me feel sick to my stomach. Those, I realized, I would do better without, so I chucked most of them even if I thought I may need them later. For me, most of the important papers can be found through the proper channels later on once I'm past this mess... things like receipts from items now broken or lost, or anything that made me mad, I threw out. Old letters from businesses long gone or personal things that were already taken care of and wouldn't need to be revisited again were thrown out.

It wasn't very physically taxing but was emotionally draining. I had to push myself to keep going. I tried to sort the piles into things that had to be taken care of soon, personal happy things like photos and letters, and papers that I thought were important and necessary to keep (for real instead of imagined). The rest was garbage.

One thing that was quite difficult for me to throw out was reading material that I wanted to eventually read. Lots of it held useful or interesting information, but I had to face the facts that as things are, it is highly unlikely I would ever get to read them. I rationalized, but this time it was for my benefit instead of to my detriment, that most of the information could be easily found again on the internet. I could also go to the public library to read the books there, not bring them home until my house is done and I am organized or it will just be lost and I will have more fines that all add up.

In my house, the three worst areas are clothes, dishes/food, and papers (including books, photos and magazines). So those areas were the ones I wanted to tackle.

At the end of the first day I managed to put three big black garbage bags filled with paper trash out of my house. My tendency is to keep the garbage bags inside the house when I sort so it's not so noticeable that there's a problem but I am past caring what others think and just care to fix the problem and myself.

I completed the initial sort of all the papers that were in my room. I say initial because I know I'll have to get back to these again later on but I've done all that I can do with them for now. I had washed probably a third to a half of the dirty dishes and put them away (putting away is very important), washed and dried six loads of laundry, but had only folded about two loads and the rest were dumped onto a couch where I usually watch TV and fold. I grabbed my clothes, hot weather shirts, hot weather pants/shorts/skirts, sweaters, jeans, and dress pants. The button up shirts and dresses were hung up in my closet.

I didn't want to go to sleep with my bedroom not completed so I took the boxes of papers that went through their initial sort and set them on my couch outside of my bedroom because I knew I couldn't complete that task before bed. This feels somewhat backwards because they are making more of a mess elsewhere in the house, but right now my main concern is getting my bedroom completed.

I couldn't think too much about the rest of the house because if I let it get to me, it would just sabotage my efforts. For me, I have to have an area completely finished even down to what is in the drawers or it goes back downhill.

My clothes were all put away neatly into their drawers and hung up and all that was left to do was wash down the furniture, vacuum the floor and make my bed. Washing furniture works better than dusting with a dry rag because it actually takes away the dust instead of pushing it around.

It's amazing what a completely clean room does. I felt at peace, I felt energized, I felt thankful, happy, appreciative, young, light and creative. I didn't worry or feel guilty about the rest of the house; I just enjoyed my accomplishments for the day.

With my own space all organized and clean and my bed made with freshly laundered sheets, I showered up and got into some clean pyjamas and then I let myself relax. I lit a candle in the now safe for a candle environment and read a book that I had been wanting to read but didn't have time for. Amazing how much more time a person can feel they have in a clean organized environment. I felt so thankful that I knelt down to pray and show God my gratitude.

Gratitude had been something difficult to feel most days surrounded in chaos and clutter. I lay in bed that night with a smile on my face and remembered something I had heard when growing up, and again just recently. I let it sink in as it went through my mind over and over again. "Every day in every way, I am getting better and better." Something my dad used to say. This mantra has helped me very much this past week. I have found myself smiling so much more. Things really are changing for the better for my family and me.

Chapter 4

WIPING OUT THE CANCEROUS CLUTTER

May 16, 2010

This is the day that I almost washed every dirty dish in the house, every pot and pan and every article of clothing. I think I ended the day with close to a load left of each. Remember that the day before, while I was cleaning my bedroom, I also spent time in between washing loads of laundry and washing dishes by hand (we have no dishwasher). I spent most of the day folding clothes while watching movies. When all surfaces were filled, I took the time to pick up the piles and put them away into their proper organized drawers before going back to fold more.

I can't stand when clothes are just shoved into drawers with no order as to what goes where so I took the time to take everything out of the drawers in each bedroom and reorganize them in a way that makes sense to me. Socks and underwear always go on the top drawer for me, and then sleep wear. Bathing suits can go in with the socks and underwear if there aren't many, or they may need their own drawer. Then t-shirts, dress shirts, play clothes or workout clothes, jeans and work pants or play pants (if for the kids).

I think that covers everything. Oh sweaters usually need a drawer even though they take up so much space. I also bought a canvas shoe box the other day to hold my dress shoes.

I don't know yet whether that is a good idea or just another thing that will get wrecked before it gets used. Right now it is filled with my dress shoes and is placed under my bed so I think it's useful. *(It turns out it was more of a waste, but I forgive myself for that and move on to what works better for me).*

I love old chests to store material or extra bedding or seasonal things in. I love the look of them. Again I don't know if they are helpful to me but I think they are. I did go out and buy pretty containers the other day for the linen closet inside my bathroom. I actually use it for toiletries cleaning supplies, towel and rags. I organized the bottles into the bigger fancy wooden boxes in a way that looked nice to me. The kids already have them disorganized but not as bad as it was. It won't take much time to take care of it and still have it look neat and tidy in the closet.

I think what I will have to do is look at where they "reorganized" things and work with that. If something else make sense to them then I should consider it, as sometimes what they do makes more sense than what I do. I love the containers for organizing, but I do have to be careful not to go overboard and buy more than what I need or should have. I have that mentality where if something is good, then more of it is better. This is one of the ways I will have to change how I think and how I see things.

I made a delicious pizza the other day for my family from scratch. I put very few ingredients on it and it tasted better for it. If I had put on ingredients the way that I put things in my house, it would have tasted gross. Living this way not only clutters up your living space but it ends up cluttering your mind as well. It's quite messed up because though you feel ashamed of it, you don't really want to change it. In a strange way it brings comfort.

I remember looking at my kids' bedroom floor. It's always been covered in clothing. Usually it is the clothes I've just finished cleaning, but it's mixed in with the dirty laundry as well. This happens daily even when the floor has been picked up and empty to start with, it ends covered. It makes me angry to see after all the work I put into keeping them clean only to have them spread out all over their floor again days later.

I felt angry, but then to me it also felt like a birds nest, all cozy. It is a tiny bedroom and they had both of their beds tightly packed into the room leaving only a small space to walk. Sometimes the clothes would get piled so high that they would be almost level with their beds. I know it is not healthy to think of it as cozy. Underneath and inside their clothing piles could contain numerous insects as every summer we have an ant infestation. If they happened to throw an apple core or something into the pile (which has been known to happen) then it's all the worse. That is what I have to think about because that is what will drive me to change the situation.

I know that my writing could be hard to follow right now at the beginning because my thoughts are like my house; cluttered. I want to see the change in my thinking as there is a change in my home so I don't intend to edit much of what is written.

So to review, I started out wanting to clean my bedroom for a peaceful place of rest and renewal to go since I wouldn't have the internet or cable to use as distractions and escape. My bedroom has been kept clean. I had to dust with a damp rag a few times because pollen came through the window and covered everything.

I also knew that if I washed every single article of clothing/material and cleaned every dirty dish, then the house would feel cleaner without having to touch anything else.

Once those things were done, then I could begin to tackle the rest, but without the laundry and dishes completed, it would be like trying to swim to the top of a waterfall starting anywhere but the top.

This day my kids came home from their dad's. The littlest one was home by 5pm and the older kids were home by 7 that evening. I was hoping to have my goals accomplished by the time the youngest came home but I was just shy of finishing up.

It would be my middle daughter's birthday on the Tuesday coming up, and she had just celebrated it with her dad, so I let my youngest daughter help me wrap some of the presents. We had no tape (that I could find) so we used a glue stick. Thankfully the wrapping paper had been put into my bedroom sometime since Christmas so that was easily found in my clean bedroom. It wasn't too much of a chore to wrap gifts and then clean up the wrapping mess, and then we made cupcakes for when they returned home so it would feel more birthday-like.

I hadn't planned on having a celebration until Tuesday, but my daughter had called and strongly hinted at wanting cupcakes and a little celebration. When the birthday girl came home we gave her one gift at a time. She was happy, but I felt a bit sad that I saw I had bought things that I know will soon add to our clutter. I bought them before this mission to clean, or maybe during the time the seed must have been planted in me. I guess it's always there. We hoarder/cluttered-up people aren't oblivious to the mess and the problem. As I've said before; it's complicated.

Chapter 5
A LOOK INSIDE

INSIGHT

There are numerous reasons for being this way and usually only a few reasons why we stay this way when we want to change... a couple being: we don't truly believe we can change, and we don't know how to change even though we want to.

Maybe it's similar to any bad habit/addiction. There are various stages. At times, we don't even want to change. We like how it is. If no one else were bothered by it, we would not even think of changing nor see the need to. Then at times we can't stand ourselves for it. We feel angry at letting it get to this stage... angry at everything and blaming everyone (usually just ourselves but sometimes family members or others as well)... we feel angry and disgusted. Sometimes we can become super motivated and actually get things cleaned up but then fall back into the way things were. Sometimes we lose faith in ourselves. Sometimes we lose hope.

Then sometimes seemingly out of the blue it happens that we just know we are ready for healing. No one but ourselves pushes us to this stage (and maybe some gentle prodding from God). This is the stage where there is no lying to ourselves about the state of things. This is when we will do everything necessary, including face the painful things in our lives that got us here, to climb out of our deep hole before it becomes our grave.

This climb is going to be the most difficult thing you've ever done, but you just know it will be worth it to be free. Every reason you've stayed this way or fallen back into old patterns, you will have to look at with open eyes. Every step upwards you'll find something that could send you back to the bottom if you let it. You'll see things in your journey that will flood you with memories and you'll be paralyzed till you can shake it off and take the next step. You'll have to feel that vulnerability, the sorrow, and the hurt; let yourself feel the joy as well.

You'll have to remember people and places and events that were buried underneath your clutter or fat or drugs or whatever vice you've grasped on to in despair. You'll have to remember them and then let them go. Don't be afraid to feel the pain that will come, but don't hold on to it any longer than necessary. Give it to God. Whether you believe in Him or not, accept the gift of Him taking your burdens. You shouldn't have to carry them any longer.

See, when we hold on to these burdens, that is when we can fall back down. Those burdens are heavy when held onto. Sometimes you only stumble back a few steps before you let it go and surge forward because you see that light at the top that you yearn for. You don't need the hole any longer and you know that once you climb up out of it, you'll be the person that you always knew was there inside of you. The one you dream of being but couldn't because you were drowning underneath whatever you have cluttered your life up with.

This is the same whether you clutter your life up like a hoarder with things, an alcoholic with drinks, a fat person with unhealthy food (I'm fat, and I know I didn't get this way by steady daily exercise and a healthy diet.

This part now bothers me. It was a way I bullied myself to call myself fat. Even though I am heavier than what is healthy for me, it is not nice or even accurate to call a person "fat" because there is so much more to a person than their dress size. So I apologize to myself and I apologize to all of you for this. I'm leaving it in though because perhaps what I am saying now will help others), a gambler with a ticket, a sex addict with sex... oh I could go on and on. There is no end to what we people use to escape life to feel temporary pleasure instead of living it to find happiness in something more permanent and real.

I think once you get out, there may be times when you wish you could just jump right back in the hole for a bit, particularly when something in life brings fear, or when emotions run high, but you'd never want to stay there again. Life is too good to live it inside of a grave.

MORE INSIGHT

I think the reason that it doesn't necessarily help to have someone else come and clean up for you is the same reason that it won't necessarily help to have someone else feed you or make sure you don't do any more drugs. You have to come to that place where you are ready to heal. **You** have to do it. It can help to have outside help but some people need to do it alone. Certain people tend to do better when they have no one else do it for them. They just have to get up, dust themselves off, and trudge ahead. No one else can feel the emotions for you. You have to do that on your own. There are many steps that no one else can take for you. No matter how many times someone else cleans up after you, you won't change unless you take responsibility and take your own action. I would like to see the people in these hoarding shows in six months or a year.

Just cleaning up the house doesn't solve the problem. If it did, I'd be fine by now, many times over. I have some wonderful people in my life despite all of my eclectic collection of walls I've built up. They try to help and they do love me, but they can't change me no matter how grateful I am to have them in my life and for what they have done for me.

This is my mess and I need to climb out in my own time. This isn't a free ticket to say do what you want and not worry about fixing your own personal situation. We all need healing. So how long do you really want to keep picking at the scab and opening the wound? At some point, don't you want to allow yourself a chance to be healed and free from everything that has shackled you down?

HEADS UP

Alright, I've spent enough time on this computer this morning... it's time for me to get back to work. It is now noon for me. My plan for today, Monday, May 20, 2010, is to launder all of the bedding that was found and not quite fresh and clean, I need to make lasagna, I need to do breakfast dishes and any dishes I dirty during the day from eating and making supper.

I need to put away all of the laundry that is left, I need to clean the floor of the kids room, then vacuum and bring in the wooden chest that their father and I had built together 14 years ago. It's been sitting outside long enough now (2 years but it's made of cedar so it's still good).

I haven't decided what should go inside that chest yet. *(The chest is now gone. Its lid was broken and it was just one more thing I had been holding on to that did not improve my life by keeping.)*

I think that will be enough to do because I have rehearsal tonight. Thank you for taking this journey with me and I hope you set this book down where you decided it belongs (hopefully not the garbage, and hopefully somewhere you can find it easily again) and maybe throw in a load of laundry or dishes too!

Oh I almost forgot to mention that I'll be drinking some water and eating an egg sandwich on whole wheat bread that my son made me for lunch. (*He was only 10 years old at this time so this was really impressive. The kids could see I was trying, and so they were helping me in whatever way they knew how. Once you begin, you will most likely start to see others pitch in to help you wherever they can).*

This morning for breakfast I had two glasses of homemade kefir (similar to yogurt... a strong probiotic) with a tablespoon of maple syrup in it. I think I'll have a glass of homemade Kombucha with my lunch as well (look it up, fascinating stuff).

Update: June 7, 2010

I didn't accomplish everything I had written here for goals for the day. The lasagna didn't get made yet and the cedar chest is still outside but it has been emptied out and I still plan on making lasagna. *(I have since learned that it is better to make small do-able action steps/goals to accomplish each day rather than a huge list where only a few will get done and the rest go on the next "to do" list. That way you make a plan and keep your word so that your belief in yourself grows and you know you'll keep your word and do as you say you will do. Also saying I "need" to do things that weren't actually needs, like I need to breathe, impeded my progress. Words are powerful. It was better for me to say I "want" to do something.)*

I washed the laundry but there is now more because my littlest got sick with a bladder infection so she's had some accidents and had thrown up. I'm pretty sure I finished the dishes that day as well but since then there have been a few setbacks where nearly every dish in the house has been dirty at once and all the counter space has been taken up by them for days at a time.

Some dishes on the counter today may have been there a week. Dishes have been washed nearly every day. They haven't been completed every day. Setbacks are normal, and they are a part of the process. Learn from them.

The lunch was delicious from what I remember and we are on a new batch of Kombucha already. I also just remembered that I wrote an update within this time on paper that may never find its way into this book. The topic was not too pretty, but this entire book subject is not too pretty is it.

I am opening up to an ugly side of my life. Perhaps I will share and maybe it will help someone else. *(I don't remember what I spoke of here. It could be the following, or may have been something else now lost. If I find it, I promise I will put it in future publications).*

What have been some of your setbacks?

_____
_____
_____
_____
_____
_____
_____

What can you learn from them?

_____

_____

_____

_____

_____

_____

_____

_____

_____

_____

_____

_____

What adjustments will you make so that next time, that same setback will not get in your way?

_____

_____

_____

_____

_____

_____

_____

_____

_____

_____

Chapter 6
STUMBLES, BACKSLIDES AND GETTING BACK UP

June 7, 2010 (Three Weeks Later)

Well I knew it wouldn't be an easy process. I'm not there yet but I can report that my bedroom has been kept clean every single day except today. Ironically it got messy while we were working on the rest of the house and I didn't tidy it all up before I left the house. I can see that I'll have to be somewhat obsessive compulsive in order to keep it from going back to how it was.

Before I sleep tonight I'll make sure everything is back in order or I risk it all. It sounds overdramatic for some, but it is reality for me. I have been here too many times to ignore how it all starts and how easy it is to fall back into old patterns. It's such a mental challenge and I have often sabotaged myself in one way or another, either by giving up under the overwhelmed feeling when I am beginning to lose control of things or by fooling myself into thinking I can get to it later. I think I can safely say this is similar to how addicts feel when they are sobering up and getting clean.

"Getting Clean" is a nice coincidental term but it all makes sense here. Maybe one of the main differences between an addict and someone like me is that an addict hides all of that mess on the inside (or at least tries to), whereas I wear it on the outside from my body to my house, it's just extended outwards.

I still have concentrated mostly on my bedroom and the kids' bedrooms. I haven't been beating myself up about the rest of the house. My rule has been to keep our bedrooms cleaned daily and before going to bed. I've noticed an interesting effect that it's had on me; I am starting to be more comfortable in a clean environment than a messy one. I have started to despise the dirt. I have become repulsed by the mess. I've noticed the bugs; the ants and flour beetles that have made themselves at home in my home and it sickens me. I see the filth and it makes me on edge. My kids have borne the brunt of these feelings when I lash out and they are there to catch it.

I flip out when they begin to complain that they have to do chores. I just cannot let us go backwards anymore. I can't live like this anymore. I need us all, as a family, to make this change. I know it starts with me and I do have to be firm in enforcing the change in them as well, and I have to find a way to do it that won't ruin the relationship that we do have.

I can't flip out and lose my cool on my kids. That isn't the right way to handle things. Just when I do see how messy I've raised my children to be I can't be complacent anymore. I know that if they stay how we are, if WE stay how we are, we'll never get out of this hellish dump that our home has become, and every home we ever live in will become, as it will follow us wherever we go.

I do love my bedroom now. I keep the door opened during the day. It's beautiful to look into and see a clean floor draped in sunlight from the opened window and feel the breeze that gently puffs out my curtains from the wall and into the bedroom. It looks so peaceful. Now I know that is what I want my whole house to feel like. I do believe that I will get there. I finally do believe it.

My cleaned up bedroom is converting me. It has made me realize that I am capable of keeping an area cleaned daily and I can keep on top of it. It has made me uncomfortable amidst the mess and chaos and I know that I'll be unable to have the mess continue forever. This all takes time and I am not rushing myself. I need gentleness and understanding right now... even from me. As long as I don't allow things to go backwards for too long and I keep my bedroom cleaned then I'll eventually get there. I plan to have the cleanliness grow like a cancer (only a good kind) or maybe I should think of it more like the mess is the cancer, and I'm pushing it out starting from my bedroom.

My ex-husband came over a few days in a row about a week after I started this. He told me I should just get a bulldozer. This is after I had been making my progress. I was actually quite proud of how far I'd come in my own time but his comment really deflated me. In the past I would have allowed it to drive me to the computer to give up. This time I see it for what it is. It's a bit of a stumbling block that only has to be as powerful as the power I give it.

I don't know if he realizes how much his words had harmed me in the past and how much they do now, but I can't let it get to me anymore. I know my path and I won't be led astray this time. I can't let any excuses in. Excuses are just another wall that stands between me and my freedom from all of this. Sometimes doubt creeps in, but it doesn't swallow me up anymore. Doubt was my whole existence regarding this illness before, but it is only because I wasn't allowing myself to see the alternative. I felt powerless, so in my mind I was powerless; but that is not the truth.

The truth is... people have been overcoming "impossibilities" since our existence and the biggest thing standing in the way of doing and "I can't" is our belief in being able to do it. It sounds corny, I know, but it really does have truth to it. Impossible you say? No, I'll show you that it IS possible.

I don't know if you've ever had someone believe in you or have never had someone believe in you, but regardless of how many have or haven't, the most important person to believe in you is yourself. It is wonderful to have support from people who care, but until you believe in yourself, other people's belief in you doesn't have its full power.

It's like if you imagine an enormous boulder in a field and your friends are there with the ropes trying to move it... as soon as you start to believe in yourself, that rock starts turning into a feather and little by little as it changes, and as your belief grows, it gets easier to move. Their support is wonderful, but it really only starts to help when you start to believe in yourself.

This is something that you have the most power over one way or another; either to say things stay how they are, or for things to change.

It's late and I had better head to bed soon. This late bedtime will have to eventually change as well but for now, it was nice to sit down to write. So to check in, my bedroom is mostly cleaned and will be cleaned before I lay down in bed, dishes are mostly done, there is probably a load or two left which ideally should be done before sleeping but I'll allow it for now since I'm not at the stage of having my dishes completed every day before bed.

Laundry is a bit behind but the difference now is there is only one big laundry hamper full of dirty laundry instead of four overflowing onto the floor and taking over our dining area, bedroom floors, bathroom floors and living room floors. All the clean stuff has been put away neatly into their places in an organized fashion.

So despite what my ex-husband thinks, I'm not doing too badly. I would say my word for this moment and stage is "Progress". I have also been getting out more and have begun to incorporate exercise into my days (but only just begun). It's enough of a start that I feel terrible for eating all the fast food I've eaten lately because I've been busy, and I have determined to put a stop to that. Goodnight and I'll see you next time.

HEADS UP

I'm going to tidy my bedroom before sleeping. There are a few things on the floor and my bed isn't made. I think there are a few things in my bedroom that don't belong there so I'll take them out and may or may not put them away depending on if they have a place yet or not. I'll brush my teeth, change into jammies, and get a good night sleep. I don't think I'll read anything. Writing was good enough and it's almost 2 am now. TTFN as Tigger would say.

Chapter 7

MAJOR BLOWS

August 19, 2010

I can't believe the last bit I had written in here was 6 days before my father died. There has been some writing in a journal but nothing on the computer. I have a lot of catching up to do. There are a few things I want to take note of.

It is driving me crazy lately because I did do my quick tidy solution of getting a few rooms totally cleaned by removing pretty well everything that doesn't belong and stuffing it all into boxes in another room.

I had probably half of the house superficially cleaned and vacuumed. Every single day it gets to be a disaster again between cleanings and it is exhausting but that is because I am not taking care of the underlying problems.

There is still too much stuff that doesn't have a home. Plus I don't have rules in place to keep our home from becoming messy and dirty again so it backslides in no time at all. It feels like my kids don't care about all the work I am doing and it makes me want to give up. Perhaps I should just remove everything excess from the rooms and put them in the shed if there is space, or throw it out. Then when they have nothing to make a mess with, it won't be a problem any longer.

Sadly my beautiful room is a mess again. It has been since the night dad died. I know it can't be good for me and probably contributes to this feeling of helplessness or wanting to give up again. I'm sick of it. I don't feel like going to bed; don't feel like cleaning because all the effort is sabotaged daily. It is like fighting a monster that refuses to die and no matter what I do to scare it off, it keeps coming back every single day.

The only way I can conquer it is to have everyone who lives here working together instead of against each other. I also will have to look carefully at myself because sometimes it is me who sabotages things without even realizing it. We still have so much purging to do because there is way too much stuff for this house. It can never be cleaned completely with all these extra things with no determined space for them and no room to designate a place for them. It will always be chaos until we have only as much as what will fit in the space that we have.

I think I have to start with cleaning my own room instead of my children's rooms. It should be their responsibility now to clean their rooms up, not mine. Even my youngest can keep her room clean. If she refuses, then the toys or whatever is making a mess should go. Well enough of this. I have to go to bed. I probably should clean my bedroom before going to sleep even if it takes me all night because this is the time I have to get it done. Sleep can wait I think. This may not be the best thing to do, but I want to stop putting up with it. I want to stop making excuses, even reasonable ones.

There is so much to add here and I will return hopefully sooner rather than later. When I had this to keep me somewhat accountable I was making progress. It is too easy to slip behind now. If I can fix my room up again then I have space to heal; this time from something more than my hoarding.

I know dad would wish that for me and be proud of me for being the strong woman he raised.

Strong doesn't mean forgetting him or ignoring that he has died. It just means not letting me drown under the emotions. It actually could cheapen his death, all he means to me, and my love for him if I use this sorrow as an excuse to feel sorry for myself or to let things go or to put off all that I need to do.

Sure it is difficult, but I need to do it for him as well as for us. He would hate to be the reason for me to backslide or giving up. *I love you dad, and I want you to be proud of me.*

INSIGHT

Don't sabotage yourself because ultimately it all comes back. It is not worth the short term pleasure in exchange for poor long term results. Sacrifice the short term for what comes as a result.

For example:

- **Diets:** Long Term = healthy weight and healthy body with more energy vs. Short Term = yummy food/toxin ingested then forgotten everywhere but on the scale.
- **Cleaning**. Long Term = nice healthy peaceful environment vs. Short Term = relax / lazy time.

Just do it and stop sabotaging yourself with excuses or temporary pleasure.

I want to cry for the past me here. Grief is such a difficult time. I was hard on myself when I just needed love and comfort from someone. Since I had shut myself out from people, I had no one but my children to comfort me, and it was too much to put on a child. I feel so sad that I pushed everyone out of my life so that I had to deal with my dad's death alone.

Yes what I said had merit. The way I said it was not loving or supportive. So for now, current me gives past me a nice big hug and tells her she's doing great with everything that she's been given. I tell her I love her and I am sorry she's hurting so much, and that I know dad would be so proud of her for everything she's done and is doing.

August 6th, 2010

It will be a constant fight and struggle if I wait for the kids to do something all because I did something for them. Why not just take the initiative and clean for them because: a) I love them, b) to show by example, c) because they are good kids, d) they do things for me, etc. Then once things are getting better, it will be easier for them to help out and we will all be happier. I need to remind myself of what they do to help.

Anya made lunches today and supper the other day and she babysat. Dylan took Emmy to the park for hours to play and did so happily. Emmy washed her hair and is going on the potty and staying dry and clean :o). Selah is working hard to get good grades and works at being a good kid and good person in general. So they do give me plenty of reasons to be proud of them and to want to do good for them as well.

It doesn't always have to be about whether they have cleaned up and done chores or not.

How have you been hard on yourself unnecessarily?

_____
_____
_____
_____
_____
_____
_____
_____
_____
_____

How could you be supportive to yourself instead?

_____
_____
_____
_____
_____
_____
_____
_____
_____
_____
_____
_____

Chapter 8

GROWING THROUGH GRIEF

August 7th 2010

My dad died last month...well almost two months ago now. It is hard to keep track. My room didn't take long to slip up. I think it was the night I found out he died that it started. It started with my clothes not being put away and my bed not getting made. Then I had to pack in the midst of heavy grief. I could not even think to pack properly so my clothes were strewn all over my bed. I packed too much.

Dad died only a month and a half before his 59th birthday from a brain hemorrhage. He was in Mexico so that is where I had to go to take care of him after he died. The first dead body I had ever seen was my own fathers, naked, in a Mexican morgue. I was all alone. I didn't speak Spanish... though I listened intently hoping I would begin to understand, and they didn't speak English. They needed family to identify him and I was the only one there since my brother got deported in Mexico City for lack of a passport, it was unlikely he would be able to return in time to do it himself.

Dad taught me many things in life, and now, in death, he was still teaching me. He had been 10 months into his dream of living on his boat and sailing the world. He was sailing the Baha Haha and was nearing Guatemala border when a storm with strong winds hit and he was forced inland. Next would have been the exciting sail through the Panama Canal. Instead he was forced to slow down.

I think it scared him enough to modify plans to see us. He was due to take a break to visit my brother in three days. The plane ticket was already bought and the arrangements were made for someone to take care of his boat while he was gone and in a month's time he would be coming to visit me and the kids. It had been two years since I last saw him. I love my dad dearly and think the world of him so he is a lot to lose for me.

I had been doing so well and felt myself really reaching for happiness for the first time in a long time and at times I fully grabbed hold of joy. Life was good. My house was progressing and I felt in control, making steady improvements towards my goal of home being clean and organized. I was performing in a play coincidentally called "The Death of Me" and was enjoying that. My kids were coming with me to the theatre at night while I performed and would either watch the other one act plays, or would play at the nearby park. So we were settling into a nice routine together.

The last night I performed, before the show, my youngest daughter and I were standing at the window three stories up... her on a chair and me just beside her. She pointed out two ladybugs lying still on their backs. I explained gently that "yes, they are dead honey," then quickly added "or maybe sleeping" when I noticed her bottom lip start to quiver. Then not a second later a black crow flew directly across my vision from left to right. It made its impact on me and then was dismissed.

That night we just got back home and I was tucking in the kids when the phone rang. It seemed weird that anyone should call so late. It was mom. She asked how I was and said I had better put the kids to bed and she would call later.

I was lying down with my youngest when the phone rang again. I expected my mom but it was my brother, Dan.

"I have some bad news Angel." He sounded shaken up. Last time I got a phone call like this it was about my aunt who had had a heart attack but that didn't come to mind this time. "Shoot... NO!" I thought.

"Dad?" I just knew right then. An unwanted knowing before he could even finish.

"He's gone"

"Noooo....." Then grief flooded over me and I cried in a way I never had before. It was like my body wanted to turn itself inside out starting with my face.

Dan gave me a few details but I really can't remember the details of the phone call. Mom had come over while I was still on the phone and I was oblivious to everything. I don't even remember saying goodbye to my brother. Mom stayed long enough to give some comfort and advice to get some sleep and see that I would be alright and then went back home.

Once the kids were back in bed and mom had left, I pulled out my photo albums. I needed to see dad again, to pull every memory I could from those photos. To bring him back somehow. Dad was so lovely, so unique. Mom might have described him differently, but there is no one else I'd have rather had as my father.

When he was younger he saw a lady with hair down past her bum and so he never wanted me to get my hair cut. Mom had to sneak in a trim every now and then when he was away at work. He used to brush my hair 100 strokes before bed while we looked out at the stars when I was around 3 or 4. Then we would find a star to wish upon and watch for the shooting stars.

I remember sitting on his lap reading from this enormous family bible. He would open it up to a random page to read from, like that was God talking to him. I loved the artwork in it.

Sometimes he would sing. I loved to hear him sing. He had a great singing voice and a knack for making up songs. I remember when I would get scared at night after a nightmare and he always let me fall back to sleep safely curled up next to him with his arm as my pillow. This was all before my parents split up. He was the best dance partner hands down. Every woman loved to dance with him. They didn't even have to know how to dance and he'd make them look like stars because he knew how to lead.

He has given me an abundance of memories and experiences but selfishly I want more. I am not ready to be fatherless. Mom told me that when I was born, he said "well I had better get my act together now that we have a little girl." He was always a gentleman, protective, and flirtatious with the ladies once he was single. His ocean blue eyes and charming smile won over many hearts though his belonged to mom till the day he died.

Somehow in the midst of my memories and mourning, I came back to the room I was in, looked at the clock and figured 3 am was still a fine time to call my brother. We talked for probably an hour and then both decided tomorrow would be even harder to face without sleep. I curled up under my blanket and we hung up.

My tears didn't stop for the sleep my body succumbed to. In the morning through my wet eyes I saw a very sad and puffy-faced me in the mirror. My eyelids were so swollen from crying I barely recognized myself. I looked awful but somehow it was comforting to see. My daddy died. I didn't want to feel numb, I needed to be affected by it and feel the pain.

You only get one dad in life; that's it. Maybe somehow my grief could bring him back. I don't know. Death is such a strange thing. So hard to fully accept and understand.

I woke hoping it could be a dream but knowing better. If it was going to be real, I wanted to try to experience it to possibly understand better. Death was so foreign to me. Never had it been so close. It is still hard to grasp.

Dad doesn't feel dead. Not his spirit. I know his body is now gone; now transformed into ashes. I found some of his writings and one sentence that stood out to me was "to be absent from the body is to be present with the Lord." That is just how I felt, looking at his cold dead body. That wasn't him anymore. It was cold meat. It was like looking into an abandoned house. No one lives there anymore.

The kids say I am not myself anymore. I guess depression has found me again. Understandably so, but I don't think I want it to stick around. It has got me thinking; which comes first, the depression or the mess? Like the old conundrum "which came first, the chicken or the egg?" This is a question without a definitive answer. One does tend to cause the other.

I just hope to be stronger than my depression this time. I hope to work through it to a peaceful environment that might help pull me out of this darkness...eventually. Never mind the hope... I choose to.

DAD

Just last month Death surprised me;
the ease with which he slipped into my life
and made himself at home
like an old acquaintance
who thought he was a friend.

On this side
he does not smile
and overstays his welcome.

Damn you Death,
I will never understand
your awkward presence.
Mostly I wish I had not met you
nor received your gift
of this somber straight jacket.
I have no wish to wear this dress you've
draped me in then clamped shut over me,
overtaking me.

Peel back this heavy crust encapsulating my spirit.
Light is now an old forgotten chapter
silhouetting something just beyond my focus.
No lens can sharpen this image enough to
make sense of it all.
Brighten this light until flames erupt and
maybe then I can see.
But no, he is still too far to feel his warmth
through my charcoaled shell,
concealing me from all colour.
Black has painted my joy,
tainted my air.

Chapter 9

PICKING UP THE PIECES

August 8th 2010

MY HOUSE

Tonight my bedroom is a mess. The dishes are all washed and put away (third night like that in a row) and some laundry is in the wash. Most of the house is a mess because I tore it apart looking for my cell phone that I had lost the night dad died. I finally remembered where it could possibly be but that bag is unfortunately missing. It could be at my ex in-laws. *(I eventually somehow found it in between couch cushions).*

My son's birthday is tomorrow. He turns 10.

THOUGHTS

It is so strange how all this works now that I am paying attention to see it. I know that it will make a big difference if I clean up my bedroom and keep it from becoming the dumping grounds again but every time I decide it is time to get at it, my emotions become heavy as if to say "not yet."

So this is really an outside manifestation of how I feel on the inside. I am just not ready to feel better yet; but I also know that if left, I would have a very difficult time getting out of this feeling, this dark cloud, when it is time to move out of mourning. I don't need these obstacles holding me back.

When I get a nasty gash on my leg, I don't fill it with filth just because it hurts, I clean and dress the wound so that it has a chance to heal in its own time, otherwise it will introduce new problems that never had to be there. In that way, I need to clean my surroundings so that I have a chance to heal as well.

Once again, this is no disservice or dishonour to my father. He didn't have me and raise me for this. He wants me to heal no matter how much I miss him. I know that how I live(d) has also kept me from getting to spend more time with him. Again, it is selfish not to give myself a chance to heal and to live and to make the most of this life that he helped to give me. I have to believe that it can be done or I will never get there. I think deep down, I still have doubts that I'll make it. It's sad because I know that so many people would scoff at this. "What is so difficult about getting off your ass and cleaning up? It has to be done and we all have to do it." I don't know why it becomes something so emotional. I just know that it does for me.

I remember cleaning up after myself when I was very young and even wanting to be clean. This is not to blame my mom or dad but just a recollection and observation that around the time they split up seems to be when I started collecting things and having such a hard time letting go of anything and not cleaning up my space. I have two main memories of cleaning from when I was a child.

One was around the time of my parent's separation… just before actually. I was 6 years old. My mom and dad were out and my brother and I were home alone. I remember making green Kool-Aid and taking cloves of garlic, swallowing them, and then chasing them down with Kool-Aid to drown the taste. This was meant to keep us from getting sick. My brother had heard that garlic keeps germs away (and vampires too… which couldn't hurt).

I started washing dishes and cleaning up our mess when I accidentally broke a bowl and was quite upset that I had done so. When mom returned, I started crying and she comforted me to let me know that it wasn't a big deal. Then she smelled the garlic and we had to explain to her that we were keeping ourselves healthy. I guess we were before our time with this preventative medicine, but it didn't work. We both got sick because of all the garlic we had ingested. We ate so much that it came through our pores. I think we stunk for a week.

We moved often, so sometimes I group my memories together according to which house we were living in. It was this same house where mom and dad took me into their bedroom to explain to me that dad would be moving out. That they were separating. I was always an optimistic child so I tried comforting them both with "it's alright, you'll get back together."

Well my dad held on to those words for seven years, if not his whole life on some level. I know mom was the love of his life till the day he died. She won't like hearing this but it is the truth. No one ever measured up to her in his eyes. I regretted saying those words that gave him hope for years because I wanted him happy with someone else, but the 'someones' would come and go and never stick.

I remember in that same house after dad had moved out I wanted to do laundry for mom. Having watched her many times before, I was sure I could figure it out. It couldn't be too difficult. I put the clothes in, poured in one cleaner and then the other and started it up with the buttons. I was quite pleased with myself and was sure mom would be too. I knew she needed the help since she started working.

I don't remember exactly how it went but she was not happy when she found out the laundry was started for her. She ran downstairs and as she pulled the clothes out from the washer, her face got redder. She was furious, in my 6 year old eyes. She held up her brand new exercise outfit and what was once a nice black and grey striped spandex body suit was now splattered with yellowish blotches. Apparently the one cleaner I had used was bleach and that was not to be used with every load and never with colours.

That was the only time I remember mom yelling at me. I don't think she ever let me do laundry again and she still has an aversion to letting anyone else touch her laundry. I really don't know if these experiences have shaped how I am now. I am sure either parent could make a good case for the other but ultimately it is I who am responsible for how I am. I am the only one who can take responsibilities for my actions and inactions... no one else is responsible.

I did think that because my formative years were spent with dad and because he was at times a messy bachelor (ok... often a messy bachelor) that maybe it was more to do with that than anything. Then I thought that maybe it really doesn't matter the reason why or the recipe for being this way, I just need to stop it. I am, however, beginning to think that it does help to understand the process, but also important to move on from that. Acknowledge and let it go.

It would make sense that when I lost a parent from my everyday life that as a child I would try to supplement that loss with stuff; with holding on to every toy and article of clothing that was mine, even if I had outgrown it.

Every holiday that I would spend with my dad was an opportunity for my mom to purge my bedroom. I would always come home to a clean and much emptier bedroom. I do believe this made me just want to collect more to replace what was gone, even the things I couldn't remember, which is why I can't see the techniques used in the hoarding television shows making any lasting positive impact. I know I drove my mom nuts with this process and my now inability to keep my room clean and I do understand completely why she did what she did, but it did also reinforce my packrat like tendencies.

I still have dreams of going into my old homes to find my lost stuff. They are reoccurring dreams that I couldn't understand before but maybe this is part of the reason. Maybe it was harder on me than I had thought. I dream of finding my old notes, toys, clothes and coins. Usually these dreams take place in my dad's home that he lost years ago to the bank.

Often there will be piles of ancient coins that I try to stuff into my pockets to no avail. They are never there in the morning. I suppose that is an analogy to life and death. All the things we try needlessly to accumulate that make us feel happy or secure for a time will never be able to be brought with us into whatever is after death. I think this is something to think about for a while (or meditate on, to those who prefer that terminology).

Wow! Reading this now in January 2016, I think I finally understand why those dreams of my stuff from childhood are in dad's house. They represent dad. They always did. All the accumulation of things were because they replaced my absent father. I loved him so much and if I couldn't have him close, I could at least have what reminded me of him close by. I could hug my teddy bears and keep the dress he thought looked so beautiful on me.

As long as I kept them, I would have a part of him around regardless of how long it would be till I saw him again. I had those dreams because I wanted my dad back. I wanted all the parts of my dad that I didn't have anymore because my parents were separated and he lived so far away. That eventually engrained in me to find comfort in things. I could get attached to things because they wouldn't leave me. Even if they got thrown out, I could replace them. I could not replace my father. No one ever could take his place.

I don't know why my attachment was to things rather than people. I don't consider myself a materialistic person at all. Quite the opposite actually, but maybe in my mind, those things represented the people who mattered to me. I could (or should have been able to) hold on to the things and keep them in my life, but I had no control of being able to keep people in my life.

So it would hurt much less if I could have that attachment to things rather than to people who mattered so much more. How sad because the things taking over my life actually keep me from the people I love. Even from my children. My oldest daughter now lives with my mom, but not only that, the time we all spend on cleaning or avoiding cleaning should be spent together doing fun family activities or something else.

BACK TO REALITY (OR AT LEAST THE PRESENT)

Okay, enough reminiscing. It is my son's birthday and I need to make him a cake (or buy one?) I know it is smarter to buy than to make right now and then use the extra time to clean up for him. The front room and dining room would make him so happy. Maybe I should start there!

Well, after writing all of that I was able to throw out two big boxes of clothes the kids wanted to get rid of and I was having difficulty letting go of because of all the money I just spent on clothes for them. I realized it is stupid to keep them when they will never wear them even if they are nice quality clothes. It just makes sense to get them out of my house and maybe someone else can use them (at a second hand store or something).

I know later on I will want to go through the boxes again to double check usefulness or something so I'll have to resist that urge. While I am able to think clearly, I can see that it is not going to do a bit of good to get those discarded clothes again. In fact it will add to the clutter and mess and inability to have a clean home.

I also backslid three times the other week. The video store is going out of business and if I bought enough of them, I could buy them for $1 each. Since I got rid of cable, I thought that it would be smart to buy videos to take its place. Over three separate trips I bought probably 200 movies and 30 ps2 games, most of which are probably old graphics that won't hold my son's interest anyways.

I should take this as an opportunity to get used to getting rid of those we have watched and aren't interested in watching again. I wonder if I will.

This was a big waste again. I think we watched no more than two of the movies. They were cheap because they were awful, despite having won awards. Netflix is a blessing and so is the Library.

Chapter 10

PUTTING MY FOOT DOWN ON EXCUSES

August 27th 2010 (up to date now)

A materialistically overcrowded house equals a house that is next to impossible to get clean and impossible to keep clean. This is the key. It is what I have to let sink in even through my expensive learning experiences of buying hundreds of videos or books on sale. Anything that isn't a necessity at the moment is excess and that excess will get in the way of me having a clean environment.

Some notes written earlier and transcribed from a scribbler notebook on August 26, 2010.

August 5th 2010

A Few Things

1. I can't expect the kids to eat at the table and not in front of the television when I do it and the table is never cleaned.

    The dishwater will need constant changing if the dirty dishes aren't first rinsed off. That takes lots of water, gas, dish soap, and most important of all; time. It is so easy to scrape off plates when finished eating, then rinse them off with hot water and a cloth or hand as soon as we are finished eating... then washing is a breeze and dish water stays sudsy and clean for many loads. This will save lots of time and energy, not to mention probably money.

2. Make sure the garbage can always has a bag put in properly or the garbage will find its way out of the bag and onto the floor or into the can to rot and stink. It's hard to clean out, becomes smelly, and attracts bugs so take garbage out every night to avoid this. The smell will lessen and eventually be gone. Garbage stinks, especially old garbage. Day old stinks less so; older than a day is awful. You don't want that stench in the house. If it's in the house then it's on your clothes, even the clean ones. This means you stink to other people no matter how clean you think you and your clothes are.

SO IN OVERVIEW

Dishes washed nightly plus garbage taken out nightly (as well, all garbage should end up in the trash can, not on the floor or on a counter etc.) plus laundry washed, dried and put away equals a house that starts to smell nice equals you smelling better and equals less bug infestations and pests.

What I have found is that it doesn't take long to put away the dishes. So take the extra 5-10 minutes to put them away into cupboards and everything feels nicer. It is worth it. This has the added bonus that it will be easier to clean the next ones, which means there are less excuses for not doing them.

If you can't find room to put the dishes away into cupboards once cleaned then you have too many dishes or need to designate spots for them better. Don't use the cupboards for anything other than the dishes they are meant to hold. Don't keep more dishes than what your cupboards will hold.

MY PROGRESS

My room has gotten messy again since Dad died. I see when I am depressed my surroundings also become depressed. I need to make a conscious effort to fix it up again. Laundry is also back into that dangerous pattern and I refuse to go there again whether I'm in the middle of mourning and the hardest time in my life or not.

Just to keep you all updated on my daily progress (at least the days that I write in here) today my water got shut off. It isn't that I couldn't pay the bill; it's just that I was putting it off. I seem to have a block up somehow and though I know I have to pay the bills, I just set them aside to get to "later" if ever.

I guess I just hate money going out right now because things seem tight and I should know that it only hurts me more to let it go and then have to pay more money to get them to turn things back on etc. etc. but it didn't stop me from leaving it.

So wasteful for me. I should know better...and I do know better, I do. I don't even want to make excuses though I suppose it is because I am grieving. Sometimes I hate how I am. There are things about me that I like, but there are others that I really don't.

I had the worst day today with regards to dad. I couldn't talk to anyone without the tears coming and uncontrollable sobs overlaying my words so I was pretty well impossible to understand. Anyways, I paid the bill less than 5 minutes after the boys left who shut off my water. It's a shame they couldn't have come to the door and given me the option before shutting it off since I was there and I actually spoke to them before they even touched the thing.

They said if I pay today then it'll be turned back on today. That was at 9 this morning and even the overdue accounts person said it would be turned back on today, so I left for the day, came back expecting to have water, turned my taps and there was nothing. So I phoned and spent another half hour on hold till I could speak to the answering service who called the on call guys who replied that it would cost me $140 extra if they were to come tonight after hours even though I already paid another hook up fee of $110.

Then they proceeded to mention that if I don't get it done tonight I have to make sure I am home at 8am tomorrow. If I am not, they will charge me another $140 because apparently I have to be home when they come to turn the water back on. They didn't have to check if I was home when they turned it off but I suppose it is to make sure nothing floods if we had turned on taps when the water was out and didn't fix it.

Anyways I am just complaining senselessly. This won't do anyone any good. It just makes me feel better to complain about it right now. What I probably should be doing is taking responsibility for not paying my bill on time. For not having a set place for all the unpaid bills to make sure they get paid, and for being so passive (non-caring, can't think of the word) about taking care of my responsibilities because these are the real reasons I am in this situation.

I can't blame the kids who were shutting off my water because they didn't have to give me a warning even though I would have really liked one. My water was shut off simply because I didn't pay my bill and rather than jump at taking care of the bill when a warning was sent out in a letter, I set it aside to take care of later, which basically ended up being ignored.

These days if I want something done it needs to be done now or I forget what I had been meaning to do. I can't retain any thoughts lately; nothing short term. Though I do recall mentioning that I plan on cleaning up my room tonight and considering it is now 1am and I have to be up early for the water guys... hmmm, this is a tough one.

I want to keep my word, but perhaps it was not the best idea in the first place. I really should get a good sleep and be awake for the water guys in the morning and then clean my room once they have been here. Goodnight for now everyone. I suppose this will all take much longer than I had hoped it to take.

August 22, 2010 (glancing back)

It really feels a shame that less than one month after I started this with a solid determination to make these real changes to my life, something would happen so big and difficult to deal with emotionally and otherwise as my beloved father to die.

To look at the big picture, I want to say who gives a shit about my messy house; My DAD died. I don't care about the state of my house compared to him. I lost my one and only father. We may have many father figures in our lives, and even step fathers and fathers in law, but we only get one dad and as much as I love my step-father and yes, even my ex-father in law, there is a difference. My dad, no matter how he was seen to anyone else, was one of the only two perfect people alive on earth in my eyes up till I turned 18. When I look back, it seems almost every major experience I've lived was with my father.

So how can I move on from this? How can I not let this melt and evaporate all that solid determination I started with three months ago? I didn't realize till I looked at my timeline that I shouldn't feel discouraged by what feels like a lack of progress.

It was just under one month from the time I started till the time I got the phone call.

In that time, I was able to make a substantial amount of difference in my house and life. I was just getting to a place where I was having fun again and enjoying my life. I spent more time with my children and spent time doing things that I love as well as things that needed to be done and we were getting a routine (which is essential in this road to becoming free of my clutter and mess).

My floors were visible (at least the majority of them), I could see an end to my mountains of clothes, where before they threatened daily avalanches. My bedroom was kept clean and easily so, and on top of being able to cook daily meals, we got the dishes cleaned and put away each night.

Life throws road blocks at us. It happens to us all. So even through the most difficult of times, we have to at least try to carry on with those things necessary in life such as eating, sleeping, working, and cleaning. Even some laughter is essential in the midst of sorrow.

It may be months more, or even years before I am able to fully feel joy again but at least I have a chance at that joy if I continue on this path that I started rather than at times allow the all-consuming grief along with my clutter to swallow me up.

ACTION STEP

On the following page is a list of affirmations. Read through them aloud daily in the morning and at night before bed. There is also a tear out affirmations page at the end of the book for you to keep with you at all times.

SPACE CREATION AFFIRMATIONS

- I get more and more organized day by day.
- Space is valuable. The more space I make in my home, the richer my life becomes.
- A space for everything and everything in its space.
- I complete my tasks from start to finish.
- My cupboards and dressers hold enough.
- I believe in myself. I can do this.
- I wash my dishes daily.
- I become free by letting go of stuff.
- I trust myself.
- I live with self-integrity and say no to what I don't want.
- My memories come from experiences, not from things.
- There is abundance in the world.
- Space is freeing.
- Better things are yet to come.
- I look forward to the future and enjoy my present.
- I love my life.
- I deserve to be healed.
- I deserve a clean environment.

Chapter 11

GROWTH... SIX YEARS LATER

THE ALL OR NOTHING APPROACH

January 2, 2016 (almost 6 years later)

It's the New Year, January 2nd and the only reason I am writing right now is because I had set the intention to do so before noon. Despite my desire to help myself and help others, I know that if I hadn't made that commitment to write 1000 words before noon, all of my good intentions would have turned into guilt at not having written anything. It just wouldn't have happened. I would have found anything else to do other than what I say I want to get done.

It would be nice to get this done, to write a book that will help myself and help others.

I'll also admit... to have completed a book from start to finish would be pretty cool. I want that. I have about three others written part way by "Old Me" who didn't know how to commit and finish a project. "New Me" knows this book is already done though I have not yet completed it.

Before now, I would have sabotaged that want by any means possible. Most likely I'd have unintentionally opened up an IPhone game to play. It's that part of my brain so hell bent on keeping me safe by keeping everything as is that tries to hold me back.

Wanting something isn't going to be enough. Wanting leaves you with more wanting. Committing, and taking action is what will get you what you want.

I know this book that you now hold in your hands, yet at this moment is incomplete (as I write it) is done already because I have made that commitment. Nothing will stand in my way of completing it. I've made a plan, and I stick to the plan until it is done. That's how I know it is complete. I now just have to do the work to get it there.

With the all or nothing approach, as I've proven to myself time and again, "nothing" would win out. Think of this book. I can only complete it one chapter at a time, one paragraph at a time, one sentence at a time and one word at a time. The letters take care of themselves in the words, but they still have to be typed.

It will get completed because I have committed to writing 1000 words per day a minimum of 4 days a week. I am striving for 7 days a week but I know that there will be days where I don't write anything. I know myself and allow that concession. I let myself be where I am right now. When I am at a place where I've got the four days consistently down and succeed at that, I may look at increasing it, or I may leave it where it is. I'm sure you can see the analogy to healing the hoarder.

Almost six years have gone by since I began this book and the project of "me". When I first decided to bring this back out and finish it, I wondered how I could. Six years went by and I hadn't written a word on it. I hadn't been documenting my progress. Was there even progress? A quick look around my house shows that yes, there has been a great deal of progress, and that look also shows that there is still room for improvement.

A glance into my memory reminds me that there have also been relapses through the years. Yet there's a smile on my face when I think about it all because I see how far I've come and I know that I will go so much further because of that commitment I made years ago.

I never gave up. It is absolutely imperative that you do not give up. No matter how many times you fall or slip or tumble right back to the start, you need to get right back to it and keep on going. As my dad used to say when I was learning to ride horses, "When you fall down, you get right back on that horse. No matter how many times you fall, you get right back on it the second you can stand and you will conquer that horse. You will triumph." The longer you wait to get back up, the harder it is to start again but you still must do it.

I'm in the middle of my journey. I now have other self-improvement projects that I am working on, though this is still something that will always take some work. After all, a home doesn't clean itself. I now know how much easier it is to take care of my home with less inside of it. Now when I shop, if I am mindful of that, I will buy only what serves my goals so my house won't get to how it used to be. I also know that if I am not mindful of it, like anything, I could end up backsliding by coming home with too many things to clutter it up.

Here is the difference; I will never allow it to go back to what it was. The biggest reason for that is that I will never give up. I don't look at it like I always have to struggle with this. There's no end to how much better I can be as a person overall. I love to strive to better myself every day in every way.

It isn't that it becomes easier; it's that I have become better. It's easier because I am stronger, I've got better strategies, I've got belief in myself. I've become more accustomed to a nice clean home than to a home covered in filth and mountains of stuff. It's easier because once I made that decision that I will conquer it no matter what, I no longer had to deal with all the mind chatter telling me I can't. If you hear the mind chatter after you've begun, just tell it to get lost, or a nicer way, you can tell it "thank you for sharing" and get back on that horse.

This is a beautiful journey, and so much more enjoyable the nicer my home gets. Yes it does still get messy sometimes and does still take work to keep it from getting too bad or from staying a mess. It still makes such a difference to have my bedroom my sanctuary no matter how my house is. I now have a diffuser with water and essential oils in it to make it even more inviting. I have a little writing table in the corner where I sometimes write with my laptop. It motivates me to keep the rest of my home the same, or clean it up so it gets back to that.

Despite my progress, I have to be careful inviting my mom over to visit. She usually goes through everything and inspects cupboards and rooms and all the hidden spots. She points out the dirty spots on the walls. I know she means well but it makes me feel like what I have done isn't good enough until it is all spotless all of the time.

After this book, if she reads it, she will know that what helps the most is for me to celebrate the improvements... even when those improvements are seemingly tiny to anyone but me. I notice what I am doing that is working and I see my overall progress. I also notice that it isn't all done and I know there is more to do. Some days the house looks worse than others, but I know that I am still making progress and will continue to do so.

This is where I will find my balance and my success. I love my life now. I don't focus on the mess. I have so much else in my life to experience and enjoy. Life shouldn't be about just zooming in on all the problem areas.

You may have heard that what you focus on expands. When you focus on the mess, it expands. When you focus on the problem, it becomes bigger. Instead, when you focus on what you love and enjoy, and on the progress, you get more progress and love.

When you see how great it feels to make that progress, and celebrate it, you want more of that progress to celebrate. It feels great. It becomes more of a joy instead of a chore.

What are some ways you have progressed from the start of this book?

_____
_____
_____
_____
_____
_____
_____
_____
_____
_____
_____
_____
_____
_____

What ways can you add beauty and enjoyment into your life?

_____
_____
_____
_____
_____
_____
_____
_____
_____
_____

What do you have to celebrate?

_____
_____
_____
_____
_____
_____
_____
_____
_____
_____
_____

What would you prefer to focus on in your life?

Chapter 12

LOVE AND FORGIVENESS

Now I want to tell you something very important. You may need to let it soak in and it may take a while before it fully takes hold in your life and you can apply it, so read it and know that it will come in time:

YOU NEED TO LOVE YOURSELF.

You need to love yourself exactly as you are right this moment, mess and all. You need to accept yourself how you are right now. Even if you are not satisfied in staying this way, acknowledge yourself and your struggle and your journey. This is you. This is the best you could do with what you've had thus far in your life with the mentality you've had and the troubles you've had and the hurt you've had.

Don't be hard on yourself by saying you aren't good enough, or that you should be better by now or anything other than where you are right now. You can push yourself to be better. Just don't beat yourself up for your current situation. It doesn't help to do that.

Instead, look yourself in the mirror and tell that beautiful soul "I love you". Really feel it. Even if you don't believe it yet, say it and be open to getting there. Now keep looking at yourself and say "I am sorry". You can elaborate or not on what you are sorry for... that you are sorry you got yourself in the mess you're in, that you are sorry you let it go this far, or any other reason you are sorry, but tell yourself that you are sincerely sorry.

Then I want you to tell that hurting person in the mirror "I forgive you". If it doesn't stick, say it again. Look yourself in the eyes, and say it as many times as it takes to begin to feel it. Lastly commit to yourself that you will heal and you are worth healing. Look yourself in the eyes and say "I commit to getting better no matter what it takes because I am worth it." Repeat this every morning, and every night.

Now be gentle with yourself. Change your definition of "getting better" from having everything perfect to every day you improve. This month you are better than last month, even if no one else can see that change. This year you are better than you were last year.

Your backslides will happen less often with more time between them and when they do happen, they last shorter periods of time... and you notice them coming on quicker, so you can change direction quicker. You may not even see the difference for a while, but if you are making that effort to improve, and taking action to getting better, you will be making progress. Progress is the secret, no matter how little. If you are heading in the direction of your goal, even if just a step, you are closer with that step than you were before.

Then celebrate how far you've come. Celebrate even the small wins. It doesn't have to be a party, but can be, for the big wins or small. You are worth the celebration. Celebrate and reward yourself in a way that you can feel good about. When you reward your progress, you'll see more progress. This can be difficult to get in the habit of doing, but it is important because it reinforces your positive actions and turns them into habits over time. It also brings with it a good pride... the kind that allows you to see that you are worthy of a good life. You are worth more than what you've given yourself. Eventually you will learn to love yourself.

The start of me loving myself was when my mom, as she often did, told me that I have to get my home in order for my kids, that they don't deserve this, that they are worth more than that. She was tearing up. I knew she was right. I knew, and I tried. I tried so many ways, so many times. I knew my kids deserved better.

I knew they were worth getting better just for them if not for me. I was doing all of this for them. I tried so hard. It just felt like a lost cause. I didn't know how.

But then she said something that really hit me. She said "Angel, YOU are worth it. You don't deserve this." It hit me like a sledgehammer. I couldn't breathe for crying. I knew mom loved me. I knew she was even proud of me at times. This was the first time I'd ever heard her say that I didn't deserve this.

I knew my kids deserved a clean home and a happy life but I must have, somehow along the way, begun to believe that I didn't. So no matter how much I thought my kids deserved better, because I thought I didn't deserve better, it never changed. I thought they would grow up and leave, but I didn't deserve better than this. It wasn't a conscious thing. I wasn't aware of it at all.

This Christmas I read a testimonial from a beautiful lady on a diet forum on Facebook... a doctor at the start of her journey. I read her testimonial and it was littered with jabs at herself. I recognized the bully in her because it was the same one that had been inside of me.

Though she was a stranger, I felt a need to reach out to her as I would if I saw a bully on a street picking on someone. I'll share my message that I'd sent to her (next page).

"The bullies of your past do not have to be carried into your present. I just read your testimonial ... and I see myself in some things. I would like to share something I recently had an epiphany about but still struggle with. Reading your message I was really able to see it. You and I both bully ourselves. I can tell there are many wonderful things about you and it isn't a matter of lack of will power because you certainly need determination to succeed and become a doctor.

You and I both could benefit from learning to love ourselves and accept ourselves fully as we are, and be supportive on our road to bettering ourselves. To be kind to ourselves and embrace all that we are at this very moment. That doesn't mean we don't want to change some things or that we will stay just as we are, but right now, for now, we are perfect.

Some of how you spoke about yourself (and I've done the exact same thing) would be so cruel if someone else said it to us. Yet because it is coming from us we accept it. We shouldn't. Every person out there has things they want to better about themselves, but that doesn't give anyone a right to say they aren't enough.

Love yourself. I will do the same. Hopefully this letter is alright. I know we are strangers. You're beautiful, intelligent, and funny, which all came through in your letter, but it also comes through and was stated that you didn't love yourself. You can do this. I think more importantly is that you deserve to love yourself and be kind, understanding, and gentle to yourself. The bullies of your past do not have to be carried into your present. Take care. - Angel"

In the past, whenever I wasn't perfect, I chastised myself without even being aware of it. My friends would tell me I'm hard on myself or mean to myself but I didn't see it. It wasn't until this summer when I was at a self-improvement camp that I realized it.

I was about to go up on a high wire and to the spotter (person who held my rope to let me down when it was time) I said, "I'm heavy" with a smile. Instantly I felt how it would feel had someone else said it to me. She looked at me with compassion when I said it and I think that's what made me realize what I'd done. I cried because seeing it that one time opened my eyes to see how mean I had been to myself all throughout life. I finally understood what my friends could see.

She was so beautiful with me and helped me, gave me support and encouragement. It affected me so much that I whipped through the obstacle determined to stop the bully inside me and love myself as I am right now. I went so fast that the person on the other side who I was to meet in the middle and go around, didn't even have a chance to begin.

She'd only just reached the top of the pole. I didn't notice anything else around me until I finally heard my name being shouted by everyone. I looked down and they all clapped for me and said I could come down now. At a different camp three months later at a similar obstacle, I talked with the lady about what I would be letting go of and what I would embrace. I let go of that bully inside and embraced a love for myself. That love has come and has shown itself as well within the last three months.

This New Year's Eve I was at my mom's and she and my step dad were verbally picking away at me as they often have in a light hearted teasing way, and usually I just think they are only wanting better for me and it's them showing me that they love me, but this time it was so weird... like I was waking up to it. Yes, she and my step-dad were doing it out of love, but they didn't know it was only hurting me and making me feel like, "oh that's just me... ridiculous, lazy, incompetent me" as I usually would, in an accepting way while I would also laugh at myself and my "silly" ways.

This time it was as if I'd awoken to what it really was and who I really am, not the person they were poking fun at. I am capable, I am hard working, I am intelligent and I am a wonderful woman. I'm not a child. I don't need them telling me I'm not doing things well enough. I don't need to do things as they tell me I should. I am a 40 year old woman. I'm not a child. I am living life the way that I know is best for me, mistakes and all.

Children are allowed to make mistakes and learn from them. That is how they learn best, and we should remember that it is the same for adults.

It took a few minutes for me to do something. I listened to my parents say what they were saying. I watched them laugh (I'd have normally joined in), and I felt the hurt. I allowed myself to feel the sting of their words and laughter.

Almost stunned at what to do, I said "Stop! I am 40 years old. You may not be proud of me and where I am right now but I have come a long way and I am proud of what I've done and how far I've come. You may not be, but I am. You may never be proud of me but I think you should be.

I may not have everything together but I am proud of my progress and all that I am doing and all I have done." and then my step dad apologized. My mom didn't really. I didn't know what she thought but what mattered right then was what I thought.

It wasn't how I wanted to begin the New Year... feeling unworthy. The evening didn't end there. I wondered if it would and I did feel like going home but I stayed and we talked because they matter to me. I knew they didn't mean to hurt me.

It's just how we used to do things and they weren't trying to be mean or hurtful but this new me, the part that loves me, wouldn't stand for it because I won't stand for it from myself any longer either, and so I felt the pain that should come from a loved ones taunts... whether they meant it in a light hearted loving way or not.

There are better ways to love someone and show that love. As mom told me many times in the past "you get what you allow and accept in your life," and I wasn't allowing that any longer.

I do love them both, and I was happy that I got to see them and spend some time with them. The next day mom called me "sassy pants". It wasn't in a mean way. More like she was proud of me. At least that's how it felt.

We all have strengths and weaknesses, and that doesn't make us a joke or incapable. It just makes us human. All of those weaknesses have potential to become strengths with belief in ourselves and the work to get them strong.

The ability to laugh at one's self is a great trait, but the ability to belittle one's self is not. That needs to end now. We are all worth more than that.

Sometimes it is a fine line and until you can tell what the difference is, perhaps it's better to just keep standing up for yourself or at least give yourself the same amount or more of praise for your accomplishments as you do laughter at your mistakes.

Also, it doesn't matter the size of your accomplishments to get the praise because it sure doesn't matter the size of the mistakes to get the laughter and sometimes ridicule, does it? Time to start being nicer to ourselves and each other.

It's nice to see that me loving myself really is taking hold now. So much so that I stood up to my own mother and step dad whom I both love and respect very much. What they said did hurt me. It did affect me, but now I see it is more about them than about me. I am doing well. Not only do I deserve this, but I am capable and am worthy of them being proud of me, whether they feel that pride or not. I do. That's what matters most.

As an afterthought to this, I know my mom and step dad love me very much and they are proud of me for many things. I bet she will even be proud of me standing up for myself from her once she reads this and understands. I love them both and mom has given so much to me in my life to help.

The most important things she has given me are love and acceptance of all that I am right this moment. That love from a mother is irreplaceable. The acceptance allows me to accept myself. It allows me to let it all go and move on to healing because she loves me however I am.

Have you ever felt belittled by others or by yourself? Write those times down.

_____
_____
_____
_____
_____
_____
_____
_____
_____
_____
_____
_____

Now think about how you can move on by forgiving them and yourself and write down those ideas.

_____
_____
_____
_____
_____
_____
_____
_____
_____
_____

Chapter 13

2016 PROGRESS, SETBACKS AND INSIGHTS

MY PROGRESS THESE DAYS

For the first two days of the New Year I began with completing my "get done before noon" list. I wrote my 1,000 words here, called my ex-mother-in-law and wished her a Happy Birthday, and took my dog for a walk outside in the fresh air. I felt so human and so normal. I spent a good deal of time listening to audio courses while organizing my kitchen cupboards. I switched the pots and pans cupboard with my small appliances cupboard, went through all of the Tupperware-type containers, and got rid of all the extras (with the exception of my juicers. I have two juicers. One juices really quickly, and the other juices greens slowly. I also have a third that is my daughters and I am storing it for her until she is more established with where she is living.

I realize how much that sounds as though I am making excuses. It does all fit in the cupboard though so I am ok with it. I was amazed at how much room it opened up to organize. I have one completely empty deep drawer that had been overflowing before. All of my small kitchen appliances fit in the cupboards instead of being on top of the countertops. My pots and pans are so organized and I even have extra space. I've been eating broth that's been simmering on the stove for two days so I'm keeping healthy overall as well. Life is good.

SETBACKS

Setbacks happen just as often now as they had in the past. The difference is how I handle them. I am a different person in many ways. I've learned some great tools, and I know the importance of persisting through the setbacks. Still there are times that I allow it all to get to me. Usually that's when I haven't been taking care of myself, if I haven't been getting enough sleep, exercise or time outside in the fresh air. Also if I have been eating junk foods, it all affects how I react to outside difficulties.

I've had a couple of nights this week where I have not been able to sleep. Right now happens to be one of those times. I thought it best to be productive during this time at least. Lack of sleep leads to bad choices like poor nutrition and partaking in unproductive activities like smart phone games or Netflix.

It also leads to saying yes to what does not support my goals and no to what does support them. In other words, the dishes did not get done today or yesterday. The action steps I had written out did not get completed. I blatantly disregarded all of what would have gotten me closer to my goals like a stubborn child. I remembered them, yet I intentionally chose to fill my day with other immediately gratifying, yet self-sabotaging activities.

One thing I've learned this year is that there are no failures, only feedbacks. My initial reaction to writing this all down is to feel shame and anger towards myself yet that does not get me any closer to my goals. It won't help me. Instead, I will take it as an opportunity to learn. What can I learn from my behaviour? I know how important it is for me to get at least 8 hours of sleep at night, which means getting to bed early. I felt wide awake earlier despite being sleepy all day long.

I got to bed early, but have been unable to sleep. I have noticed that on days where I've gotten cardio or other exercise, I have been exhausted and fallen right to sleep at night. So it would be good to begin incorporating a daily exercise regime with a schedule, healthy food, and exercise. Fresh air also helps so perhaps a nightly walk outside would help. On that note, I would like to get some sleep. I'm feeling sleepy again so now would be a good time. Goodnight and I'll see you next paragraph.

Write out some of your own setbacks and the lessons they give you. Write out what you can learn from them that will help better your life.

_____
_____
_____
_____
_____
_____
_____
_____
_____
_____
_____
_____
_____
_____
_____

So here is the thing. We have had a good 15 years of living with a system of being messy and very little time in those 15 years creating and sticking to a system of being clean.

We can still get the house to disaster state in record time. Everyone blames the next person and none of us take responsibility for our own part in getting it that way.

Really it doesn't matter who did what or why it is that way. What matters is how much do we all want it to be neat and clean? Usually cleaning falls to the one whom it matters most to, or when I get frustrated or determined enough, I enlist their help.

What works the best is when I get determined and enrol them in the process. I set a time limit that they can help, a half hour to an hour a day, and I stick to that time whether the work is done or not. That way the next time I ask for their help, they are more willing and there is less of a struggle to get their cooperation, which means we are all more productive and happy.

I had my room and most of the house cleaned recently. My bedroom had just got spotless and washed down but I had one junk drawer, a catch all, and two boxes in my closet that were making it imperfect, so I took everything out of the drawer and set it on my dresser top to go through, thinking that if it is all out in the open I am more likely to finish going through it. Instead, like a cancer it grew until my entire room became the dumping grounds of disaster once again.

I realize that I do better when things look clean and orderly even if there are some places that still need work or I get complacent, or discouraged.

I think this time it was discouraging because I had worked on everything to make it nice and then I sabotaged it by taking everything out of a hidden spot to out in the open where it looked awful.

I did the same sort of thing with a diet recently. I had lost 37 lbs and finally fit into my favourite jeans from years back. I was proud and liked what I saw in the mirror. A couple days later I was bloated, slipped on my favourite jeans only to find that they didn't fit like they had days prior. From that moment on, unintentionally I went off the diet. I made all kinds of excuses.

My favourite one was now that I know I can succeed in losing weight; I can just do it again later. I just weighed myself today and I have gained back 21 lbs. not two months later. It was through Christmas, but still, that is not what I worked so hard for, working out for 8 months steady and then dieting for 4.

How bad do I want it? That is what I have to ask myself. Why do I want it? I have to make that so clear and so strong that it is more painful to fail than it is to keep it up... which also means that I have to keep that reason on top of my mind.

Which way would work best? I will have to see what works best for me, and you will have to see what works best for you. It may take some trial and error.

I know it will take persistence and commitment just like my commitment to write. It will also take daily clear intention of fixing these broken patterns.

What runs your life... excuses or results?

_____

_____

Which would you rather have?

_____

_____

Take a moment and answer why you want this for your life?

_____

_____

_____

_____

_____

_____

_____

_____

_____

_____

_____

_____

_____

_____

_____

Chapter 14

PATTERNS AND SHAME

PATTERNS

I have noticed some negative patterns that I tend to follow. My room gets messy and I stop taking care of myself. When that happens I go to bed late every night which meant less sleep and I get sleep deprived. I waste time on IPhone games. I feed my body unhealthy junk food. I almost can't call it food. I should just call it what it is... a slow release poison.

I spend more time in my bed than I should. I avoid the world and I slip down into that spiral of depression and disappointment.

That is not how I choose to live my life, but because I didn't choose anything, it is what I let happen, until I got so fed up with it that I put a stop to it. I snapped myself out of it... sort of. It isn't an instant shift where all is awful one minute and all is well the next, but the mindset can be pretty instant.

The moment I said to myself "alright, enough is enough" I made a shift to get better again. I took steps back in the direction of what is important to me.

These slips do happen. The trick is to have them less often, and for less time, while the time between them stretches out to as long as possible. Break the pattern... and introduce new patterns that are positive.

Take some time to write about your own patterns you have noticed in yourself. Write down the supportive patterns that lead to a positive life and write down the unsupportive patterns that lead to things falling apart.

_____
_____
_____
_____
_____
_____
_____
_____
_____
_____
_____
_____
_____
_____

I broke the pattern this time with a shower. It is amazing how much more human I feel after a shower. It's embarrassing to say that I have times where I fall into a "feel-sorry-for-myself" state where I let everything go, including my hygiene. Well let's face it, this whole topic is embarrassing and shameful, but it doesn't have to keep you or me down in the gutters and sludge of self-pity.

On that note, perhaps it is time I brought up a difficult topic: the embarrassment and shame in front of others when it comes to hoarding.

Once you've written out the unsupportive patterns, write down ways to break them and create new patterns that support your success. Commit to those new patterns.

_____
_____
_____
_____
_____
_____
_____
_____

SHAME

I don't know the intent of my aunt and uncle when they took a photo of my home at its worst state and shared it around with their friends and my family members who I hadn't seen for years. I don't know if they thought it would help me when they brought out that photo at parties to share with their friends and laugh at my issue on more than one occasion, or feign concern so they could feel better about themselves... but I can say my reaction to finding out about said photo was not one that my mother expected when she confided this in me.

She expected me to be angry and hurt, and I have to say I am more-so today but back then I just felt I deserved it. It's not like they photo-shopped it. That is actually my home and I did actually allow it to get to that state. "No apology from me, it's just how I am and I deserve the ridicule because it is, after all, a real and true photo of my home."

I felt shame, and I felt I deserved to feel that way. I had tried many times to fix it and was incapable. At least that's what I told myself. Why shouldn't they laugh at me and make fun? Today I feel that anger rise when I think about it. How dare they go into my home when I am not there and take photos of it to ridicule me? How dare they sit in judgement without taking any time to try to help or see what is going on with me? How dare they laugh at my deepest wounds that have materialized in material mess?

It may have been a cry out for help but more likely it was outside evidence of all the infection of anguish inside. There were some times when these relatives helped or showed concern, but somehow that all feels pretty insincere when I found out about their malicious laughter at my expense and the photo they took to prove how much of a disaster my life had become. I wonder if it made my aunt feel like a better mother since her perfect older sister whom she had looked up to had a daughter who was such a mess.

It makes me even more angry when I think back to when I was a newly single mother, separated from my husband and father of my three children, working full time for the first time in my life and trying to hold it all together and not doing too bad at it really. Then going to college full time to make a better life for us all, getting on the deans honour roll and then getting a letter in the mail from social services saying it has been brought to their attention that my children are at risk and living in squalor and they will be coming for a visit to check on them in a few days.

My house wasn't even bad back then. It wasn't spotless, it wasn't clean or organized, but it was not squalor or unhealthy. I was a busy single mother figuring out how to take care of us all while going to college full time.

I wondered who would do that to us. Who would call that in? No one even came to visit us. No one stopped by to check on us or see how I was after separating from my husband. How could they possibly know how we lived? Sometimes my kids went to school without socks, but they always had a good breakfast, lunch and supper.

There were some extra boxes and things in the front entrance for a good month, but they were things that my ex-husband had brought back and I didn't have the time to get to them to sort through.

The dishes may not have gotten washed daily or even every second day back then and the floors needed washing, and sometimes the clothes were left too long in the wash before being put into the dryer, so they had that sour smell to them, but we were in no way living in squalor.

I had actually been feeling fairly proud of being able to get such good grades in college as a single mother of three young children and paying my bills and mortgage on my own with only $650 from my ex per month, student loans and work as a tutor. It wasn't lots, but it was enough to make it doable.

Years later I discovered that the person who called social services and reported me was the same aunt who took the photo of my home when it was in actual squalor, laughing with whomever they felt like sharing it with as if I were some joke.

The guise of someone who cares but doesn't can inflict more pain than anyone who is clear with how they feel. All of this from someone who showed me concern and made me feel I deserved being laughed at.

She called social services at a time when I was actually feeling good about myself and my accomplishments. It was quite a blow. Back then I was not strong enough to have it slide off my back. I was newly single and didn't have someone I could lean on for support or talk to about this other than my dad. I called him and he came to help. It affected me for quite a long time. I am not sure if I could let it slide even today, though I wouldn't let it stick.

Now I know that when people judge and laugh and poke fun at the gashes and open wounds in our lives, we can't start poking along with them. We have to stand up for ourselves and realize that we are worth more than that and put a stop to it, or at least eject those people from our lives.

Despite all our faults, there is so much good inside that we haven't acknowledged. We deserve more than that despite the mess we live in. We deserve love. We deserve compassion and understanding. Most of all, we deserve to be allowed to get better. We deserve faith in our ability and worth to eventually get out of the mess we've built up around ourselves.

If no one else believes in you, at least believe in yourself. No matter how long it takes; believe in your future clean, orderly home and your ability to get it that way and keep it that way once you learn the pattern and systems of being a neat, organized person.

It starts with belief in yourself, and from there it takes learning from those who have been in your shoes and have gotten out of them so you know it can be done. It also takes learning from those who successfully live the way you would like to, day by day. Yes it feels shameful having this in my past. It feels shameful having my bedroom messy right now because it reminds me of how bad it had gotten and stayed for so long.

It doesn't mean I am worthless or a joke. I am not a joke. I am not trailer trash. I am not a hoarder. I am Angel. I am not fully all the things that have happened to me, nor the things that I have done in my life. I am not where I live or have lived. I am not what I drive. I am not what I do for a living. I am not any one of my traits solely. I am me.

Those other things can all be changed. What's done is done, and is not what is. The past is not who I am today. It might be something about me, or rather something about who I used to be, but it is not who I am, nor who I plan to be, therefore it is not something I have to carry shame for any longer. It happened, it was something I went through, but it is not where I am now.

Even if you are still in the midst of disaster, if you have made the commitment to do whatever it takes to get yourself out of it, you are no longer there either. Not really. It's already in your past. You can do it! So can I.

Write any thoughts that come up for you after reading this section.

_____
_____
_____
_____
_____
_____
_____
_____
_____
_____

Chapter 15

IT'S ALL PERSPECTIVE

MINDSET

January 12, 2016

Mindset is everything. This is the same day as before, only after I gave myself a mental kick in the behind and shook off the self-pity.

It started with a decision that I'd had enough of my mental state and it was time to change it and get some things done. Once I did that, I thought about what would help me begin to feel better the quickest. I decided a shower would make the most impact on my state, as I had mentioned earlier on. I dressed up nicely after that and brushed my hair and teeth. Just the basics of grooming that can be so difficult to do when in that darkness.

I felt so much better right away which led to a domino effect of goodness. I wrote out some thoughts and got caught up on my commitment to write 4000 words per week, then got the kids to help me for a half hour while I made us a really nice healthy and simple meal of rice, brussel sprouts and dumplings.

My oldest daughter still living at home watched a movie while she folded the clean clothes then put them all into their proper rooms. My youngest daughter got in a nice warm bath to get ready for bed.

My son helped me get dishes going in the dishwasher while I cleared the countertops and put everything away that was on them, and then washed them down. I got the sink full of hot soapy water with some clean dish towels laid out on the counter to set the washed dishes on. I began with the largest pots and pans to make the biggest dent the quickest, which it did. Supper cooked while I cleaned up the kitchen.

I realize that to most people that would have been a strange few paragraphs to read, but to people who have troubles with cleaning and keeping a tidy home, I hope it will give a pattern you can follow. That is something I wished to find all these years... a system of cleaning, step by step, clearly laying out exactly what I had to do to get a clean home. My mom was very clean, but somehow I failed to learn how she did it. It is not something that comes naturally to me, but I am figuring out what works best for us.

Once supper was ready, we all sat down to eat at the table, freshly laid out with a clean table cloth. I asked my son to put his phone away, and we had supper together like one of those perfect 1950's television families except it was more fun and we lacked the man of the house. I don't think there is any correlation there. After supper we all cleared the table and they rinsed off their dishes. It's not totally clean in there yet, but I think it could be by tomorrow. In a perfect world I would have stayed there until it was all complete, but I am going to be happy with what is and perfection can come later.

I got my youngest daughter into bed at the time we had both decided on yesterday, and since she was so good about it, I laid down beside her and cuddled for a half hour while we talked. She had the diffuser going with some relaxing essential oils. We used Black spruce so it smelled like a forest and Christmas.

Her room is all cleaned up from the weekend when I helped her clean and organize everything. There is a soft light in her bedside lamp that gives a warm glow. She now sleeps in her bedroom. Before, she didn't want to be away from me so she slept in my bed. I tucked her in, kissed her goodnight, and then went to see my son in his bedroom.

I sat down on his bed while he worked on his homework and we had a nice talk as well. I helped him a little with his art project until it was time he went to bed. Then texted my teenage daughter downstairs and asked if she'd like to be tucked in as well. Turns out at almost 18, she feels too old for that. We exchange a few texts since she doesn't like people coming into her room in the evening, and said goodnight.

I can't tell you how beautiful tonight was. I feel so at peace. It was just perfect for us all. The kids each got some one on one time with me and we all got to bed at a good time. I'll be asleep before midnight, which is an accomplishment for me. I feel really good. I think I've begun to find the system and pattern that works for me... one that I can follow every night.

It's amazing this is all it took for me to go from feeling so down that I couldn't get myself out of bed, to this blissful smile and heart bursting with love for my family and my life. I want this for my family every day. To you reading this, I want this for you too. It's been too long for most of you... it's just a hunch I have. You deserve to feel this way too.

Goodnight, sleep tight, don't let the bedbugs bite you in the night, and if they do, swat a few and they won't bite no more. That's our adapted family version we made up one night. Thankfully we've never had bedbugs so it's just a silly rhyme before bed.

Use this last section as inspiration or something from your own life or a movie that made you feel all warm and fuzzy and comforted.

Write out a template for your dream evening routine.

_____
_____
_____
_____
_____
_____
_____
_____
_____

Write the pattern and how it will make you feel to live that. What does it mean to you?

_____
_____
_____
_____
_____
_____
_____
_____
_____
_____
_____

January 16, 2016

I moved my bedroom around today. My bed was directly across from the doorway which made it feel cramped and closed off. I liked it at first because of the appeal of small cozy (cramped) quarters that had been comfortable for so long.

I am changing. I see that now. It hadn't felt comfortable for sleeping ever since I put it there even though I liked how it looked. I felt more claustrophobic than I ever had before. There was an awkwardness to it which, in terms of Feng Shui (which I've recently been reading about) results in bad flow of energy called Si Chi which from my understanding means dying or decaying energy, and though that sounds all hocus pocus or new age, it actually makes sense. The moment I moved my bed to the far side of the room from the door, it felt like I could breathe easier. I took a big sigh and smiled. It just felt better.

Work has been quite slow lately. Buyers are reluctant to buy and I've had a hard time getting clients. It actually felt like there was a block up somehow. A few hours after I moved my bed, no joke, I got a new client. I just got back from showing them a home. It's almost like when there is lots of clutter and difficulty for me to move around in my home, there is also difficulty for the good energy to flow in as well. Rather it gets stagnant and sits around being blocked until it becomes sick and tainted, like pooled water.

Not long ago I would have thought Feng Shui as silly and wouldn't work, but I am beginning to see that there are so many things we don't understand in life yet. No matter how far we have come in science and as a society, there is still so much more left to understand and explore, so I will just be open to it because most likely they know things that I don't.

Why not learn from them? Why not learn from one another? We all have something to teach.

I know that when I remove the things that block my own pathways, life feels more carefree. It's just easier to go about my day. Smiles naturally find their way to my face just as easily as my feet find their way through the hallway now. The ease with which I get things accomplished in a clean environment now as opposed to how it used to be is mind blowing. Even though I have times when it gets messy or dirty or both now, it is not the same as how it used to be.

I think part of what I used to fear is that I wouldn't know what to do with all of my time if I had a clean organized house. I imagined myself sitting on the couch, bored, being fully aware of how useless I am. The thing is... I don't feel useless anymore. I actually feel like I could do anything. I can and do make a difference in the world. It may just be my little corner of the world with my friends, family, acquaintances, and community, or it may go much further. When I remove the blocks I've put in my own way, there really is no limit to what I can do.

I am not special in this respect. When people begin to believe in themselves again and in their abilities, miraculous things occur. To those who believe in God, do you think He created us to live tiny little lives unnoticed from the world? Do you think His plan was for us to hide away under our stuff... to make no positive impact? No. I can't speak for God, but somehow it feels wrong thinking He would want that for any of his children.

We are made to do great things. We are made to create an impact on those around us and to make a positive difference. That is just too difficult to do under the burden of our possessions (interesting word) and the mentalities that keep us there.

Write out ways that you have been blocking your own success.

_____

_____

_____

_____

Take a look around you and think about how the placement of furniture could be moved to give more space and allow for better flow. Write down ideas of how you could change it to make things better. Draw out your dream room floor plan.

_____

_____

_____

_____

_____

Think about your own life and go back to when you were a child and anything was possible. What did you want to accomplish in your life?

_____
_____
_____
_____
_____
_____
_____
_____
_____
_____

What mark would you like to make in the world? What about the mark in your own life?

_____
_____
_____
_____
_____
_____
_____
_____
_____
_____

Chapter 16

DEFINING OWNERSHIP

POSSESSIONS

What really is in possession of what? Are we in possession of that which we possess, or is it in possession of us? Take some time to really think about that.

What I would like us to do right now is to close our eyes and visualize something. Wait!!! Not yet! Read this first, and then do what I've said. It'll be too hard to visualize what I'm asking if your eyes are closed before you've read it.

Close your eyes, and imagine what your life would be like if your home was completely clean. No burden of mess holding you back. You could invite people over to visit if you wanted to, and you could cook something to share together... and you could even cook it together.

You could break out some art supplies and create something beautiful and put it away easily. You could open the front door to an unsuspected visitor and if you wanted to, you could invite them inside for a visit. You could shop for groceries to create a delicious meal you saw on Pinterest, or the family favourite recipe that everyone asks for but is top secret, and then you could cook it to perfection with ease and then clean it all up with ease and have it looking fresh right after, and then sit down at the dinner table to eat it with people you love and who love you.

Maybe you have people you haven't seen in a very long time who you would like to see again. You could invite them over and have a beautiful evening shared with laughter and love. You would feel healthy and you could even exercise inside if you wanted. Heck you could take that friend, turn on some music, and dance together throughout the house! You could take photos of each other inside your home that aren't close ups, and put them on Facebook to share with your family and friends and feel proud. You could wake up in the morning, decide you want to go for a trip, pack quickly and easily knowing exactly where everything is, with cleaned clothes (because the laundry is always done), and out the door after you grab your car keys from the exact location they always are.

There is so much more you could do. Visualize what would make your heart sing in your clean, tidy, nice smelling, fresh home. Spend some time there really feeling what that would be like. Feel the strong emotions that come up for you. Just sit there and marinate in those wonderful feelings for as long as you'd like. I will be here when you return.

Now, when you open your eyes, please don't be discouraged with what you see in your home right now, because what you visualized is what I want you to focus on from now on.

That is what will bring about the massive change. That is what is on its way if you decide that is what you want and if you've decided to do the work to get it. You can get it.

Take the next ten minutes or however long it takes to write down what you saw. Write down in detail exactly what you saw, what you felt, what you did, the emotions that came up, the people you'd have in your life, the actions you'd take, the things you would create, the inspiration that came up for you.

Write it all down freely. Don't edit anything. Don't judge anything. This is just for you. It will keep you on track and give you hope and encouragement when you feel down or discouraged. When you lack motivation bring it out and read it again.

_____
_____
_____
_____
_____
_____
_____
_____
_____
_____
_____
_____
_____
_____
_____
_____
_____
_____
_____
_____
_____
_____
_____
_____

Visualize it again or visualize something new that's come up since then. This is what will pull you through those times when you doubt yourself.

If it isn't strong enough to do that, please do the exercise again and allow yourself to dream. Really dream. There is beauty and joy in this life for you.

Please be open to finding it and experiencing it, no matter what you have done in life that you are ashamed of or angry with.

Find forgiveness for yourself and live the rest of your life in a way that makes it better than it is right now.

Keeping yourself down actually hurts more than just you. There is something inside of you that deserves to be seen and loved. Let it out and let it play.

There are people in this world who need that part of you. Until you discover it and share it with the world, those people will be missing what you have to offer.

If it is more about finding forgiveness for others, and you just can't find it, take a look at who your behaviour is hurting.

Does it hurt them or you more? Aren't you done hurting yourself?

Chapter 17
A LOOK INTO THE PAST

INSIGHT

I have so much to do. There's so much to get done. Guess what having a messy house does for me? It gives me a reasonable excuse, in my subconscious mind (although now conscious) to not get around to doing any of those things that need to be done.

My reasoning? The house is messy and I need to get it cleaned up. I don't have time to get to the projects and to do lists because there's all this other stuff that I have to get finished first.

Yet do I do the other stuff? No! Why? Because it is messy and overwhelming. It is the perfect self-sabotage to keep me right where I am so I don't change my life too much and become a woman who could change her life and possibly the lives of those around me. If I can't change the world, I certainly have the ability to change my own life and my own little world, but that can be intimidating and scary.

Guess what else it could be? Exciting! It is exciting to think about changing my entire life to be "super me". I know it is within my ability to become so much better and do so much more. I could actually be the woman I dream of being. She is in there.

So what is the benefit to me in keeping me where I am? There's got to be some benefit or I would not do it. It would be wonderful to have that life and be that woman I envision when I think of being my best self. Yet I continually, like a stubborn child digging in her heels, put off all that would get me to where I say I long to be. Do I not really want to be there?

Ok... it is fear. I really don't know what it is going to take to get to where I want to be. I don't know the work involved. Even so, wouldn't I be willing to do anything to get to that place and be that person if I knew without a doubt that I could be her? Yes! Yes I would. So I must not fully trust in myself. I must have some part of me that is saying I will only let myself down.

The thing is that I have discovered that I am no longer willing to let myself down. I am not giving up, even though I may have temporary defeat. I won't. I will push through to success no matter what it takes. Sometimes I just have to remind myself that I've decided to do just that and the fear will not win out in the end. My friend Barbara Ellison and I discussed this just yesterday. She had me do an exercise that allowed me to look at, and listen to the doubter in me. Where did it come from? What is it saying? She actually named hers... I don't have a name for mine but I can tell you it is really mean to me. There is a reason for that.

Here comes vulnerability time. When I was 17 years old, I had high ideals. The most important moral back then to me was to save my virginity for marriage. I didn't judge or care what other people did. That was for them to decide but for me; I would be a virgin on my wedding night. I loved the idea of saving that as a gift for my future husband... the future love of my life. It was such a beautiful fairy tale idea to 17 year old me. Only it didn't happen because I got raped.

My rape wasn't like in the movies where I was grabbed and pulled into a back alley or into the forest screaming and kicking. I don't even remember most of what happened after I accepted that drink. I do remember being in a bed with my socks and shirt on with no pants or panties. I vaguely remember a guy on top of me and I remember not fighting and kicking and screaming or even saying a word. So I thought I had just let myself down.

It wasn't until I was in my 30's that I understood what had happened. I beat myself up over that for years, and in certain ways, I still do. You see, what happened in that moment was that the trust I had in myself was broken. Something that was so important to me was gone.

I thought since I didn't fight for myself at that time when it mattered most, I never would. From that moment on, any dream that I had for myself was gone. After all, why have a dream when all I would do is fail myself? I couldn't even let the word "no" pass my lips. I didn't know that there were drugs that caused this reaction or lack of reaction. Even now as I write this out, there is this part of me saying "Are you really sure that is what happened? It was so long ago, maybe you aren't remembering it properly. Maybe you just decided to lose your virginity to a stranger."

It's so sad to think that over 23 years have gone by where I have distrusted myself with no good reason... that one situation where I couldn't say no led to so many decisions of saying no to a better me, and just letting life happen. Because of that one moment, I believed that I would never do as I say I am going to do. I would always let myself down.

The cycle of saying I would do something, and not doing it had become my norm. It was just who I was. I was always late because that is just who I was. It was the quickest way that I could show other people that I was not to be trusted. Yet consciously I thought I was one of the most trustworthy people out there.

That subconscious part of me knew differently, and I would make sure to let others know this about me as well, if not by telling them, then by my actions... little things that I could convince myself didn't really matter and didn't really hurt anyone else.

Barbara told me the story of the iceberg. That what we see on the surface is like the tip of an iceberg poking out of the water. Our subconscious mind is everything underneath the surface. All the self-sabotage and hate towards myself that came from my doubter self was growing under the surface of the water... unseen and unknown to me, yet affected every one of my actions and reactions.

I couldn't, and wouldn't tell people about those parts of myself that I was ashamed of... so the doubter in me saw me as a fraud and a fake. Consciously I felt and feel I am very authentic and honest, but then there was that dark part in me that said "bullshit, I know differently."

During the times when the old doubter became more visible, I would look at it and say no, that's not how I am, and shove it back down. I didn't even think it was important anymore because it was the past and it no longer hurt to think about those events. What I didn't realize was that even though it didn't consciously hurt anymore, it was still affecting me and my reaction to things and how I really and fully feel about myself.

Until I acknowledge what happened and apologize to myself for it... whether it was my fault or not... and commit to myself again and let that fully go, I won't be able to trust myself. The doubter doesn't care whose fault it was, just that it happened. The doubter in me can make every excuse why it was my fault like... I shouldn't have accepted that drink, I shouldn't have spoken to strangers, I should have been driving us, etc., etc.

I have to go through the process of seeing what happened, forgive myself, and be a strong woman who I can lean on, which sounds strange, yet feels right. Despite bad things that have happened, despite bad decisions I had made in the past, despite letting myself down time and again and not keeping my word, to know that I can trust myself will allow me to move on and become my full potential. It will allow me to unapologetically be who I am, committing to myself again and believing in myself again. It will allow me to start fresh and do what I say I will do, no matter what... and to trust in myself and place my own opinions above anyone else's when it comes to my own life because no one knows my strengths and weaknesses as well as I do.

The doubter needs to know it can trust me again. I felt I had given up the thing most important to me back then and I let myself down, so why would I take anything else seriously that mattered to me from then on?

That one event affected me in so many ways that I wasn't aware of. I also hadn't let myself be fully vulnerable to my friends because I was betrayed that night when the person I got a ride with left me with this stranger. I don't even remember why or when she left, but she must have. I've lived a lonely life keeping everyone at a "safe" distance... even my own children, my own family, and my closest friends. I now choose to let that go. I have to find the belief that grounds me.

Yes that happened to me, and I am now fully moving forward. I recognize what happened and can now bundle up all of that baggage and set it on the curb to be taken away. If held on to, I would never accomplish my goals. I would stay, in my eyes and mind, fat, messy, alone, broke and broken, just a little girl... a nobody.

Instead, I now can look with compassion on myself. On what happened to me in the past. On the little girl who had some really awful things happen to her that night, and many nights after. The poor sweetie who didn't even let anyone know what had happened for years... and even then to only a select few. She held it all inside to fester... with no one to trust because no one was there to save her, not even herself.

I just realized that I never had rules in my home and family as an adult because I knew I wouldn't keep them or enforce them. I still saw myself as a child. If I didn't have rules and schedules, I wasn't breaking any rules or schedules and I was letting myself down less than if I had them. I lived what that doubter thought I was capable of and deserving of after allowing something bad to happen that one time, and then many times after... in different ways.

Not anymore. I am the mom my children can believe in and trust. I am the woman I can look up to and count on. I always wanted a sister. I can be my own sister... my own best friend. Yet I can also allow others in because I can now trust myself enough to know that however it ends up, I can handle it. I can stand up for myself and if no one else stands up for me, it is alright... because I've got it. No matter what it takes, I will be the woman I believe in and fully trust and know that I am worth it.

I think that insight is worth celebrating. Don't you?

February 29th, 2016

I just reread this part, and though I love much of what I had written, and I see where I was coming from, it feels lonely when I read it this time. It is true what I wrote, but I can now also have close friends and let them in, not only because I trust myself, but because I can trust them. Not everyone, but some people are worth trusting. Yes, they may let me down at times, but that doesn't mean they are not trustworthy.

It means I get to practice forgiveness and tell them how I feel about whatever I was let down with, knowing that I come only from my own perspective. That feels better.

Think about your own doubter. Write down what it sees in you and why. Where does it come from?

Now take some time to forgive yourself for whatever brought out the doubter in you.

Let it know that you understand its feelings and thoughts, and that now you are here to make things better. That you are now showing up as your best self and can be relied on.

Write it all out so you can read it over whenever you feel that doubt. Add to it as necessary.

_____
_____
_____
_____
_____
_____
_____
_____
_____
_____
_____
_____
_____
_____
_____
_____
_____
_____

Chapter 18

ONWARD!

The following is my own template on my dream morning routine. It is not yet my habitual routine though I have tried and tested it out and I do love it. Adjustments can be made as I continue on. Try my routine on for yourself or create your own based on what you wrote down for yourself throughout the book. There will also be room to write out your own following my example.

My Magical Morning Routine (in theory)

15 Minutes Maximum

- Wake up
- Feet on the ground beside my bed
- Say "I love my life" aloud and feel it inside (care of Adam Markel of New Peaks and the book PIVOT)
- Make my bed
- Stand in a power pose for as long as I can (like wonder-woman with hands on hips or like a winner of a marathon with legs at shoulder-width apart and arms outstretched above my head and outwards).
- Have a shower
- Get dressed
- Make tea

20 Minutes Maximum

- Sit down at my desk and plan my day with intention. My action steps support my intentions and goals and my unique affirmations crafted for today (I'll use today as an example)
    - Intentions: To stand my ground as a mother, the one who calls the shots ultimately in our household.
    - Actions: Set rules and follow through with enforcing them.
        a. Emmy must complete 10 minutes of cleaning before going skating.
        b. We skate a max of two hours... if she wants to skate longer she will have to walk home.
        c. Limit my son's gaming time and follow through on that. He can play for the time Emmy and I are skating.
    - Affirmations: I am a capable mother who has it all under control.
    - Email my accountability partner/coach.

30 Minutes

- Read and learn from an uplifting book.

45 Minutes Maximum

- Wake the kids up
- Make breakfast and lunches
- Eat breakfast
- Load dishes into dishwasher
- Get kids off to school
- Feed the animals

10 Minutes Maximum

- Clean up breakfast mess

20 minutes

- Get supper planned so that is out of the way.
- Get supper started if possible (slow cooker).

Then I'm off to work.

The following is my brainstorming. You can follow my thoughts and adjust them as an example of how to do the same for you.

Working backwards that means that if the first of my kids is out the door by 7:30, I need the kids up at 7. My youngest can have a bath the night before so her morning routine is:

7:00 Awake

- Dress
- Brush teeth
- Brush Hair

7:15

- Eat breakfast
- Put plates in dishwasher

7:30

- Jacket and boots on with packed backpack

7:30

- Out the door to bus stop

Eventually I want her to be the one to feed the animals so I will wake her up 5 minutes early at 6:55... and perhaps so she doesn't have to rush, I could wake her up 10 minutes prior to that at 6:45 am every morning. This means that while she is feeding the animals, I am cleaning up the breakfast mess.

If I give myself an extra 10 minutes so I am not rushing, that means in order to follow my magical morning routine; I'll wake up at 5:35 am. That sounds terrible. So either it would be good for me to change it slightly so that it sounds better, or make it sound more appealing. If I keep it how it is, knowing myself and my body, I do best if I get at least 8 hours of sleep a night, which I haven't been getting. I would need to be asleep by 9:35. I would like to do writing or reading before bed for about an hour, so that means quiet time by 8:30 every night (to round down the number).

I could also get the kids to make their own lunches the night before, or have them help me in the mornings though their mornings are hectic usually. They really appreciate the lunches. They most likely won't continue to appreciate the lunches if I make them daily so what if I just help them and we make the majority of their lunches for the week together on Sunday. Sunday can be our day of preparation for the week. Saturday could be our day of rest.

It is more realistic if I reorganize my morning so that some of it I do once the kids have left for school. When I think about it, it feels more magical doing all of that while they are still asleep. I will try both out to see which one works best for me. I think it would be really nice to have quiet time by 8:30 every night... which means games and electronics off by that time.

Emmy would have her bath by 7:30 every night so that she is clean and fresh for bed... from 8:00-8:30 could be our time together getting her ready for bed, read to, and cuddled up so she will have a nice sleep. She will get 10 hours of sleep which is her ideal amount since she's only 8 years old.

Supper time would be good to have at 5:30 every night or possibly 6:00. Eating takes about a half hour from dish up to dishwasher. From 6:30-7:00 we could do our half hour of clean up for everyone and from 7:00-7:30 we could have our walk outside for whoever wants to come.

When the kids come home from school they don't want to do homework right away but I think it would be good for them to get it over with as soon as possible so they can enjoy the rest of their evening.

Using my method of thinking my routine through and the template of my magical morning routine, create your own magical morning routine. You know yourself and what works best for you, so keep that in mind and also be willing to push yourself to be and do better.

Write something out and be willing to try it and willing to adapt it as you see what works and what could be changed to work better. Be excited about this new creation of yours. After all, you are creating your dream life! Have fun with it.

_____
_____
_____
_____
_____
_____

Chapter 19

SCARS AND HEALING

January 29, 2016

It is interesting that something from so far in my past still has an effect on me. I had been consistently writing each week since the start of the year. After my last difficult topic, I took about 10 days off. I avoided opening this up to write. I did so unintentionally, and I realize now that it is because the topic still hurts and it took some time to recover from by bringing it up again.

I can ignore it, but that is not the answer. Problems don't go away by being an ostrich. This avoidance of writing proves to me that it still does hurt me on some level. It doesn't mean that I can't move beyond it and thrive even more, becoming stronger through it, but it doesn't help to pretend it didn't happen or affect me.

I feel that I would benefit from doing something to comfort and show myself that I do care about what happened and the awful things that have happened to me in life... some that I have not shared in this book and some that I have. I didn't have anyone to hold and comfort me after the incident. I instead had the friends who were with me (one of whom had it happen to her as well) torment and bully me afterwards.

I missed being comforted and cared for. It would be nice to get that from outside of myself, but perhaps it could be even more important that I get it from me first.

Strange as it may sound, I embraced myself in a hug, touched my face in a caring manner and physically comforted myself the way I would comfort my children because I comfort them the way I would like to be comforted. I also had the intention to be caring and loving towards myself with compassion for what happened while I wrapped my arms around me. I feel more peaceful and safe now. I think what this does is to give me healthy ways to protect and care for myself rather than all of the unhealthy ways I had in the past.

To do the same, find somewhere peaceful and private and try comforting yourself in the manner you tend to try to comfort others. Usually that is how you would like to be comforted. See if it starts your healing from past hurts.

Start placing yourself as one of the most important people in your life. Treat yourself lovingly. Stand up for yourself and care for yourself. It's nice to do this for others, but you've also got to make sure you can do this for yourself as well.

Write down your feeling and thoughts as you experience this comfort.

_____

_____

_____

_____

_____

_____

_____

_____

_____

_____

I know one of my next steps will be to begin cleaning out my body the same way I've been cleaning up my house... only bringing in the things I most love that serve my health and happiness.

I want to cleanse it from all the garbage I had been eating and instead feed it with the healthiest of food. It actually tastes better as well. By valuing myself, I see that it is also important to treat my body with respect as well as my home. I had stopped respecting my body. I now want to protect and care for it.

VISUALIZATION AS A TOOL

If you will recall back to when I first had begun this journey of healing, you may remember that there were times I would wash the dishes with my eyes closed. It made it easier to wash because while my eyes were closed, I would envision my kitchen as being spotless with a sink of hot soapy water to wash the few dishes left from supper. This gave me the energy to complete my task and keep my mind on the goal. It also gave me a template to follow with the end in mind.

How I used visualizing is not the usual way, though it did work. I used the technique before I had heard about it. Once I had, I researched and learned about the benefits of visualizing... it can make all the difference. It would be extremely beneficial to incorporate into my daily schedule.

It seems funny to say that... daily schedule. I never used to have one. The benefits to having one are enormous. It has made a huge difference to me when I do introduce bits of a schedule here and there. With it being such a foreign thing to me, I am not jumping right in with it... I would rather have it stick.

Instead I have written my ideal schedule out and am working towards it little by little. On top of changing things for myself, there are three others at home who are having their lives changed as well, so it does take more work than if it were only me.

Tonight I commit to spending five minutes before bed visualizing my ideal night time with my kids. I imagine we all sit down to eat at the kitchen table at 6:00 pm. I can picture us all talking and smiling and even laughing together, enjoying each other's company while we eat supper together.

Then afterwards my youngest clears the table while the other two get started on washing, drying, and putting away the dishes. I sweep the floor and put away anything that has been left out and we leave the kitchen completely shining and spotless.

Ideally we would all go out for a half hour walk after supper and then when we return the oldest two could do homework while the youngest has her bath. Around 7:30 she would get out of the tub, into pyjamas, brush her teeth and hair and settle into bed. I would cuddle up with a book and her to read her a story. I'd tuck her in at 8:00 and have her asleep soon after.

Then I would either help the kids with their homework if they would like help, or I would use that time to educate myself by reading a book or watching an educational film. I'd send the older kids to bed at 9:00 where they could read a book if they desired, or just go to sleep.

I would plan my next day and then climb into bed at 9:30 with a good book and asleep by 10. Then when I wake up at 6 am I would feel well rested. That sounds perfect to me.

I would like you to write out your idea of the perfect evening schedule and try it out when you can. If it takes awhile to get there, don't beat yourself up about it. You will get to it when you are ready.

It may take a few starts to get it to stick. You may have noticed my ideal times for bed and waking don't match up with earlier plans for myself. Remember it is a start... and from there, make your adjustments until you find what works best for you.

Chapter 20

DISCOVERY

February 2, 2016

My youngest daughter's birthday was a few days ago. I enrolled my all children into cleaning and getting the house ready for her birthday. They really do pull together and help out when it comes to things like this. Most days, they do not unless I ask them.

Lately I have not been getting enough sleep because two of my kids are hurting with ear aches and wisdom teeth extractions and it makes for late nights. When that happens, I am way too exhausted in the evenings to clean or delegate the cleaning. These are things I will have to be aware of and change them over time. I want to sleep soon because morning comes quickly. When I get to sleep at a good time, I wake up on my own in the morning and I can keep going the entire day.

Tonight I committed to write 1000 words before bed and I now have an accountability partner who I check in with. I promised I would get this done before bed. Please take my lead and get yourselves an accountability partner or a coach to hold you accountable.

It is interesting to think about how this book started out. In 2010, this book was my accountability partner. I didn't realize then that accountability partnering was something people had and were willing to do for one another.

I have a few sets of accountability partners for various projects... usually they are people who have similar goals to my own and we keep each other going. My writing partner and I check in with each other 6 days a week. It takes less than five minutes. Without him, I wouldn't have been writing in this tonight. The same can be done with your home. It's that added support to help you through those times when you really don't feel like doing anything. You can find an accountability partner by going to my website or Facebook page "Slaying the Dragon" or "Careful Where You Set This Down."

I have definitely hit a breakthrough in my journey. The day after my daughter's birthday party where there were 7 extra rambunctious children, I lost my keys. I thought it may have fallen into one of the child's bags and called all the parents. No one found them. I looked into replacing them and it was going to cost between $300 for a regular plain key and $800 for the smart keys... something I didn't feel I had the money for. To be quite open, I was so focused on my keys being lost and how much it would cost to replace them that I was having a bit of a panic attack.

In the past if something like this had happened, I would have torn the place apart looking for it. My home would have looked as though a tornado hit it. This time without even thinking about it, I cleaned up. I started picking things up from the party and putting them away. I swept up. I vacuumed under the cushions on the couch. I had the house almost all cleaned up again. I didn't even realize what I'd done until much later. I was so upset that my middle daughter took me aside and said, "Mom, go have a bath and relax. Take some of your own advice and stop focusing on the problem. You aren't taking all these courses to behave this way." and she was right... such a wise young lady.

She had made a soothing essential oil infused Epsom salt bath for me. I climbed in and stayed there until I stopped freaking out about how I was going to pay for new keys and how we would survive financially when I hadn't been paid for four months. I stopped worrying and just breathed in the heavenly scents. I knew Anya was right and I decided I wouldn't get out until my attitude had changed.

The water was cold when I finally got out. I stepped out with a plan. I would offer my artistic services to my friends and acquaintances as a fund raiser, and even with that I had already decided that the keys would show up. There wasn't any choice. I just knew I would find them. The art would be one good thing that came of the experience.

That's when I really took in my reaction to what had happened. Not the freaking out, but the cleaning up while I was freaking out. My habits really are changing. After I had posted a message offering my artwork, and realized how I had cleaned rather than created more mess, I decided I would go through the garbage as that was probably where the keys were.

I walked to the kitchen and noticed the towel we use for drying was on the countertop so I picked it up to put in the laundry bin and out falls the keys. It felt like angels had ascended on me singing Hallelujah... and the room filled with warm light. I swear it was a magical moment. Not only because I found the keys, but because my natural instinct was now to clean up to find something rather than tear it apart. Unbelievable! I am still shocked about that.

This really is something that can be learned. Not only learned in the mind, but in the body. It is what I now desire and crave naturally.

A couple of nights since then, despite being really tired, I have taken 20 minutes to clean up the kitchen after the day so that we wake to a clean kitchen. That's really all it takes now... 20 minutes. I didn't do it tonight, but that is why I will intentionally get to bed by 10:30 tonight at the latest.

I just have to share one little story. The night of my daughter's party, one of the moms stepped inside and said she really liked my home. She asked if she could go on a tour.

There was slight anxiety from all of my years prior when the rest of the house would be in shambles with the front room and kitchen cleaned but I knew it was alright now. The home wasn't perfectly clean and my bedroom had some boxes I was going through, but it was presentable.

We went into the kitchen, the bathroom, and the bedrooms. I apologized for the mess because I knew it wasn't spotless and I still can't really tell how bad or good it is. She said this is nothing. I should see her place. Knowing the basement was not presentable yet I kept us upstairs.

She began to mention a friend or family member of hers who's basement is completely filled. She went on to say, "She's a hoarder!" Like she was horrified. Oh if only she knew more about the lady she was speaking to. Needless to say, I did not hear the end of that story... I changed the topic. No one needs to be shamed for this. We already feel shame. If I had been more confident at that moment, I may have asked more and offered to help her friend out... maybe in time.

How funny that someone would start telling me a story about someone else as if I didn't have the same affliction... as if I were better than that person. I suppose the biggest reason I didn't want to hear the rest of that story is that I don't want to know how people talked about me behind my back.

It doesn't feel nice. I know it probably happened but I don't need to know details. All I know is that they didn't help me overcome this... I did it. My children did it by giving me a reason to change, my mom did it by reminding me that I am worthy of that change, all you out there did it, because it gives me drive to know that I could be an example to you, that by overcoming this, I could show others that it can be done. We shall overcome! So thank you for helping me on my journey. I am so excited at the possibility of helping you with yours.

While I am telling stories, I think I will tell you all about why I dug this book out again after so many years. It was shortly after attending a course called "Wizard Training Camp" that I got a phone call from somewhere in the States. I was driving and had it on Bluetooth. The lady introduced herself as a publisher for Hay House.

Well it's not every day I get a phone call from a publisher so when she asked what my book was about, I figured I had better come up with something for her on the spot, so I rambled on about how I am a single mother of four children and I have had many hardships through the years and I have overcome them and that I would like to be able to share that with others so they could also benefit from my experience and gain the courage to do the same.

I'd forgotten all about this book but I do know my life and that was the easiest thing to talk about so that is what I brought up. I forget everything I had said but it was something along those lines.

"Well that sounds like something we might be interested in, when will you have it completed?" she said next.

Again, I wasn't about to blow this opportunity by telling her "I don't know" so before I even had a chance to think about it, "6 months" rolled off my tongue. That was 4 months ago.

A couple months ago after many starts and attempts at as many different books, I found this one that I had tucked away into a folder. I pulled it out and began reading. Right away I knew this was the one I had to complete. This could be the one to help a great many people, including myself. So I got right back on that horse, only 5 and a half years later, and I began writing.

My life has changed so much since the first part of this book. I have spent the last two years taking as many personal and business development courses as I could afford to take, both financially and time-wise, and actually more than I could afford... the fact is that I couldn't afford NOT to.

It took growth from the inside out to be able to get to where I am now and it will take more to get to where I am going. It is still a journey and forever will be. I intend to keep learning and growing my spirit till the day I die, and then some if I can continue after death.

I don't have to ever worry about not being able to do something again because I know that whatever it is that I want to do, and can't do it right now, it is something I can learn and grow my abilities until I can do it. Just like that little golden book my mother used to read to me, "The Little Engine Who Could," I have to keep learning and trying and growing until the day that I get it! Then I keep on going with a little more pep in my step.

Bedtime for me! My ideal bedtime was actually an hour ago. That determination to keep my commitment has also grown through the years and I had committed to write another 1000 words. Little by little, step by step, it is amazing what we all can accomplish.

My house is currently messy. It isn't a disaster, but there is probably a load of dishes and I have three boxes of papers I wanted to go through that are still in my bedroom.

Do you want to know what I love about all of this? That it bugs the heck out of me. I just want to stay awake to clean it all up. I know that sleep is more important right now so that is what I will do instead. This means I am improving. Just knowing that I want to stay up and clean makes me happy because tomorrow I will make time to get it cleaned up.

I promise you all now, no, I promise myself that I will get it cleaned up tomorrow despite a busy day. I will make the time to do it. That makes me happy. Not much feels better to me now than having my bedroom all nice and clean with fresh sheets and a nicely made bed with a floor that I can walk on and see all of everywhere other than where my furniture sits. Goodnight all.

INSIGHT AND HAPPINESS IN THE FORM OF A KISS

As I drove my Emmy to school today she looked at her lip print on the window where she'd kissed it and remarked "This is still here?" and then proceeded to unsuccessfully to wipe it off.

"Well did you kiss it from the inside or outside?" I replied.

"Outside" she said.

What a beautiful analogy to this process where all the marks are on the inside yet are clearly visible on the outside. No matter how much wiping anyone does on the outside, if the marks only show outside because they are on the inside of a glass, then only the person on the inside will be able to fix it, and that person can only fix it by working from the inside where the markings come from.

When I've said "it's complicated" regarding this affliction, which is because although the impact on others is felt on the outside, the person living this way will not get better unless they take care of all that is on the inside first or at the same time... through fixing the outward manifestation of all that is going on. From the outside, all people can do to make lasting help is to cheer them on or give guidance for the person on the inside to heal themselves. They can't wipe it all away for them no matter how hard they try.

I still have work to do on myself to clear all those prints away to sparkling, but I have gotten it to a stage where I can now see outside. My glass now lets in the light through the prints that are left. The tinfoil has been removed! I have also gotten to a place where sometimes it is just marks on the outside that need a bit of Windex and elbow grease. Most of it now is just a matter of changing past habits and getting it done despite how I feel.

The inside has changed a great deal. When I look around now, I see my problem areas. The war is over and now it's time to rebuild. I love myself again. Last time I remember loving myself... I don't actually remember loving myself. It's almost Valentine's Day and I decided I would finish up this book by then.

This year, as every year in the last decade has been, I will be my own Valentine. Only this time I choose me and I choose my kids. It isn't by default. We are going to go out and celebrate the completion of my book and our clean home no matter where we are at. I do have that nagging inside of me that wants it perfect before I celebrate and before I finish this book but maybe it is better that I don't because perfection is part of the problem. Progression is the solution, and that is where I am... in the middle of progress.

Who knows, maybe you'll all want to take the next part of the journey with me as well and I can have a part two. I already know what I want it to focus on. I would like to have schedules and hands-on tasks to try out. I would like to have lists to cover all areas of the house and maybe even other parts of my life that I am now getting back. Then I would like to share my experience with sticking to a schedule.

I have written down so many schedules in the past and have not been able to try it even once. Yet I shouldn't beat myself up over that because I have made progress.

I still have paper clutter and I do still have things that I don't need in my house. The difference now is that I can function and still improve. It helps to remind myself of that every now and then.

Chapter 21

FLASHBACK TO THE START

BONUS... LOST TRANSCRIPT

I found that bit I had written but not included in here. I know I said I would share it if I found it, so I will, but I must warn you to read at your own risk. I'm not sure it even really adds to the book, but one of the things I have changed about myself is that I keep my word. In the past I figured a good enough excuse was just as good as keeping my word because I had a reason why I didn't do whatever it was.

This time, even though I have to talk myself into it (which is what I am doing with all I'm writing here right now), I know that since I gave my word, I have to do it no matter what. That said, I am also going to share some other notes I had written down in the same coil-ringed notebook... some exercises you can do.

Every feeling matters. Every thought matters. I need to articulate them. I bring my feelings up to the surface and articulate them. I don't let them fester.

"When you do_____,

I feel _____

It's not a bad thing... it's just feelings, neutral and no blame.

One thing I can do before bed to make me feel better about myself is:

_____

_____

_____

_____

_____

Dream for yourself, for your loved ones, for your family... not about what material things you want, but about what experiences you want. The kind of life you want. It can seem a far off dream right now but dream it anyways.

Dream it vividly and in detail. Write it down. Even if you never see that paper again, you've written it down and your subconscious mind will start acting on it.

The coiled notebook I found had in it a list of my future dream home. Ok I know I said no material things, but now said I dreamed of a home. Take that out. Dream about whatever you wish that makes you feel joyful and alive... even material things. Whether you feel you deserve them or not I want you to dream the most wonderful life in every detail.

Dream out your day from start to finish. Who is in your life? What are you doing together? Where are you throughout the day? What do you say to each other?

Back to my list. I wrote out "Can I dream for myself?" asking permission to dream. How absurd. Like I don't deserve to even dream of a better life? Of course I am allowed. You are allowed a better life and so am I.

I read through my dream… and every big and little thing on my list has come to pass other than two things. I am not married or in love, and I did not move to a farm. My life is still going so there is still time.

I met my long distance online friend. I enjoy my life. I got a camper to spend time with my kids in the summer. On down time I am able to take off at a moment's notice to travel, even for a weekend or week, even in the same province. I have a home with room to play, relax and live.

Compared to my last place it is big, but not as big as the place I moved from before then so it is just right. It is a bit bigger than twice the size of the trailer including the basement and half the size of the other house. I haven't hired a maid to clean, but I have cleaned things myself and that can still happen since the other stuff just recently happened in 2015.

I attend the gym. I have weekend camping trips in the summer sometimes. I have a nice big kitchen. I don't have the ocean or a body of water close by but that could be something in the far future. It is an older styled big home with a room for every child. There is a cozy basement though I don't use it. There is an attached garage but it feels more detached as I had written. And it has hardwood floors.

It is actually better than what I had imagined. It has a sunken living room and a pantry closet and sort of a cold room but I don't use it. It's used as a kids play room. There is a beautiful big tree to climb outside and trees we could build a nice treehouse in. I haven't seen the attic but I don't think it is useful so there is one more part I didn't get.

Some things that relate more to living on a farm I don't have but that's alright. This home feels like living out in nature because of the large yard and many trees including a vegetable garden and fruit trees (it came with crab apples, raspberries and blueberries). So that was my list all written down. It is important to write it out. I wrote it all out and then never thought of it again, yet when I look at the list, it is almost all there.

So now the bit of writing I have avoided sharing. It's as simple as ripping off a band aid right? For someone who has hid this from others for so long, I am sure sharing a lot of vulnerability with you all. It takes a lot of courage to share what I have written in this book. It takes a lot of courage to tackle this and decide to change as well, which you have begun just from reading this book. So I commend you and celebrate you. Here goes nothing!

2010   Pre-Death of My Dad

"It took one night of my kids babysitting the youngest for two and a half hours, and a week busy with work not taking that conscious daily effort, to have the house back to where I want to give up again. I came home after rehearsal to find them all in front of the TV, the littlest one sitting on the carpet naked with a poopie bum. Dirty dishes were all piled in front of them on the carpet, some tipped over.

I went into the bathroom to give the youngest a bath and clean her up then discovered a sink drain plugged up with poopie toilet paper. She had tried to clean herself up with no help and just made things worse. It was completely disgusting. The entire house smelled like poop, my hands smelled like poop. It was just gross. I tried cleaning up the sink, then her. The drain is still plugged up and I'll have to take the plumbing apart to fix it.

The other kids called me so I went to see what was up, then the littlest just ran up to me naked, dripping wet. All cleaned up but still smelling bad. It was almost bedtime and the kids still needed help with their homework so I tried to help and tried to take care of everything. It was chaos from the second I stepped in the house.

My oldest tells me she was watching Emmy but she didn't know about the poop everywhere. I went into my bedroom, my now sacred place, and stuff was all taken out of my dressers. My money was all over the bed and $40 was missing. Emmy had gotten into everything and probably hid the money somewhere in the mess. Hopefully it isn't stuck down the sink drain with the other paper. Dishes have piled up and so has laundry. Despite doing both daily I am still behind again.

Now after everyone is finally tucked in and asleep (impossible to get them sleeping before 11:00 every night and I'm going nuts) Emmy said she had to go potty as I was snuggling with her so I let her go. She came back all excited, "the bathtub is purple mom!" with a big smile on her face.

Oh great, what is it now?" I thought. Well I'd just bought new markers for the kids for school so I assumed that she dropped the purple one in it. I got there and looked in and it looked more brown to me, but thought maybe a few of them were dropped in to create the brown.

It was too dark to see through so I stuck my hand in to find the markers and had no luck. I searched again and this time my hand met with something soft and mushy. Shit! Literally! I told her to get her hand out and then pulled the plug. I tried washing both her hands and mine with soap and hot water in the sink that's all plugged up with poop and paper. It was close to 11:00 and she had to get to bed.

There was just no time to get the tub washed and her washed again, so I put her in diapers and jammies and laid down with her. Jammies didn't last long. She quickly undressed, chucked her diaper and told me she doesn't want diapers or clothes.

I really was too worn out to argue. She is now sleeping nude in my bed. I wanted to sneak a diaper on her while she's sleeping. I had forgotten about the bathtub until after they were all asleep. Well just now at 11:20 I discovered the entire bathtub bottom filled with toys and washcloths all covered with poop.

I don't know how she managed that much poop. I scooped up pile after pile with toilet paper and dumped it in the toilet, flushing in the middle to avoid a Murphy's Law disaster of a backed up toilet. That's all I'd need. I rinsed the tub out, rinsed the toys and wash cloths out... then flushed all flushables and washed myself many times with soap and water.

Then I plopped down on my bed in frustration to write this. Everything smells like poop. Dishes are all over and there's a new mound of laundry in the dining room where our washer and dryer are behind a closed door. Just a couple hours and I want to give up again. I can't give up though. It's still somewhat better than in the past.

At least this time I got rid of all visible traces of poop even if not properly washed with hot soapy water yet. The dishes won't get cleaned tonight. I'm going to get some sleep tonight instead, but first things first; I have to sneak a diaper onto my 3 year old so I don't have to deal with a peed-in bed overnight. Then tomorrow I will wake up refreshed and capable of properly cleaning up this mess. Maybe. Or maybe I'll just get all the dishes washed and put away at least.

I'm overwhelmed again, but I can't afford to give up.

Reflecting back, what should I have done differently? I don't want to give up acting. Somehow it helps keep me sane (Am I sane?). I do have to lay down some rules for babysitting that must be followed. I should have had an hour at home with them all before I left.

We should have eaten supper together at the table, then I should have had the kids to finish the dishes while I put laundry in and got Emmy ready for bed.

Once things were settled, I should have left, but not before. Dylan could have done his homework at the table while Anya took Emmy to the park. Once all that was done they should have each calmly read Emmy a story while she's in bed, then kissed her goodnight, maybe even let her watch a short film till I got home. Then I could have tucked her in and made cookies with the kids before bed. Then tucked them in, made lunches and been in bed myself to either read or write, then to sleep by 10:30. That's what I'd love.

Instead I write here with poop smelling hands at midnight, nothing done, still needing to diaper the little one. Please God help me tomorrow and help me to remember that every day in every way, I am getting better and better. Goodnight for now.

I didn't make my bed today. In fact, I went back to bed and napped around 3 hours today. Maybe this is the result. My ex came today too. Another reason I'm stressed. He always makes me stressed.

That was even stressful to read some 5 plus years later. It's hard looking back at past me. I feel pretty shitty (no pun intended) about how I placed the blame on my young kids for how it was when I returned home when I didn't even set them up to be able to succeed.

They did the best they could with what they had and what I'd given them. Anya may have even made food for them all which deserves praise and recognition. Can I look back yet and laugh at it? It sounds like some horrible dramedy where the poop joke goes on far too long. It does my children and me no good to wish I had been a better mom to them back then.

All I can do now is apologize for how it was and be a better mom today. Really I was also doing the best with what I had at the time and what I knew at the time. It's time I recognize that and be proud of what I am doing in my life now for myself and my kids. I am on page 163 of a book that I am writing on my own. That is a huge undertaking for me and something that I should be proud of, and I am. It's something I had dreamed of doing but something I almost immediately dismissed every time because I thought there was no way I would stick with it to finish, in the past. Now I know it will happen.

It's all in the mindset. We learn how along the way. I remember when Anya was going to her first day of kindergarten and she came to me crying because she didn't yet know how to read and didn't know how to do math. I told her that is why she is going to school. She goes to learn these things and doesn't have to know it all before she goes. She wouldn't have to go if she knew it all already. That's a part of the process. It's a part of our process as well.

You don't have to know how you are going to get better yet. You just have to make the decision to get better no matter what, and then start. Take your first step! This book, buying it and reading it, is a first step. Learning from it is another. Completing the exercises is another. Applying it is yet another. Then finding your own path is another step as well.

If you choose to continue the journey with me through my courses, talks, coaching or mentoring, that will be another step...one that I look forward to.

Try things out and give them a chance to work. If it doesn't work for you, try another way. Look at your life and pick one thing that would make the most difference towards living a life you love... something you can change in it consistently. Remember that failure is a part of the process. Think of learning to ride a bike. How many times did you fall? As long as you got back up one time more than the number of times you fell, you are progressing. The only time you truly fail is when you let the failure defeat you. Instead fail, adjust, and continue. Continue until one day you succeed!

Think of any time you learned something new. In the learning process, you will fail many times, and each time you fail, you learn from it. There is another way of looking at this. Failure is feedback. Failure is essential. You learn, make adjustments, and continue on. Don't be afraid of failure. When you fail, it means you are growing. It means that next time; you will be even better and go further.

Next time you will remember that the last time failure came along, you were the Victor. You conquered. You overcame. Failure was vanquished. Failure failed. It could not take you down and make you stay there. No, rather you rose up and began to believe in yourself. You rose up until you knew there was nothing that could stop you from reaching your goal.

No matter how many times you were kicked down and beaten right back to the beginning, you got back up and continued on knowing it was not the end because this race you are in is against no one but yourself. There is no beginning and no end. There is simply a life to be lived and enjoyed.

You can love this life. You can create it no matter where you are right now. You decide what you will stand for and what you will not. You decide to stay exactly where you are, or to push beyond and into something beautiful. It's up to you.

Write down all the times you kept on trying through many moments of temporary defeat until you succeeded. Write down the times you gave up. Know that it doesn't have to be the end for those times. If they still matter to you, try one more time. Then keep trying.

_____
_____
_____
_____
_____
_____
_____
_____
_____
_____
_____
_____
_____
_____
_____
_____
_____

Know that you have not met with pure defeat until you give up entirely. Maybe you gave up in the past, and now is your chance to pick it back up and make that defeat temporary. If it doesn't matter to you then let it go. Find new challenges you want to overcome.

Write out some new dreams and goals. Enjoy this life of yours! Design it for yourself, the make plans and take action on it. You can do this.

Part III

Reflections

Chapter 22

FISHING FOR MEANING

"Why" is only important when you are using it to remind you of why you are doing something that gets you closer to your goal. When looking at something you don't want in your life, and you work on changing that something, "why" is a reason. If that reason is used to keep you from doing what will bring you closer to your goals and doing things you don't want to do, that "why" is an excuse unless you deal with it. Face it, explore, and then fix it and move on.

My house is a mess right now. I started to look at why that is, but at this point it really doesn't matter why it is, I just have to clean it up. The only reason why it got this way is important is so that I can learn from it. I can look at how it got there so that I don't let that happen again, but there is no good reason for this mess today. Even if there were, I don't want to focus on that for more than a few minutes because I want to move past it.

For the sake of sharing, I see that it started when I looked back at where my affliction all began and at some of the triggers from my past. I felt awful thinking about all of that again and my energy was drained. Cleaning up after ourselves became unimportant to me suddenly. It was as if those scars from my past reached up to grab my ankle and pulled until I slipped closer and closer to that hole. I told you it was a nasty monster.

Now that I am aware of it, I have two choices. I can use it as an excuse and allow it to continue pulling me back, or I can learn from it and see the reason why, then move on from that. The person I was back then is not the person I am today either. The damaging event is the past and doesn't exist anymore. Yes it happened, but it isn't happening right now. It does not have to be my present.

So now I change my focus to look at what gives me the energy to tackle the task. What will help me to overcome all of this overwhelm? If I shift my focus and think about why I want to have a nice clean environment, and what I want my life to be like for myself and my children, it's an instant surge of energy and suddenly I am motivated to get in there and take care of it all.

I notice that as I sit here in my chair typing, my posture has improved and I feel a slight smile on my face that gets even bigger when I acknowledge it. It's magical how a shift in focus and perspective changes my entire life in an instant. I still have a mess to clean up, and I also realize that I have a house to clean up. I have a beautiful home underneath the mess. I also have a beautiful life to live and I am living it.

I have a prior commitment to a phone call that will last a half hour. It's my coach calling. After that, I will reread this little bit, turn on some upbeat music, and get to work on my environment. My coach keeps me focused on what I want so that I don't get sidetracked and swallowed up by a life that I don't want. I love my home when it is nice and clean. I enjoy being here and it allows me to do all of the activities that bring me joy. Living a healthy life is so satisfying. I don't have to look back into my past anymore. I was already there once and didn't like it then.

Time to focus more on all that I want and what I have currently that makes me happy and leads me closer to the life that I choose... rather than the one that takes me where the wind blows or that I allow to happen. The beautiful thing in all of this is that I get to design my life... as do you.

There is a reoccurring dream from my past that I would like to share with you all. It began when I was married and continued on until a few years back. I dreamt of fish. In my dreams, I was surrounded by boxes, mountains of clothes and mess in my home. In the dream, I would begin to pick up clothes and discover a fish tank underneath the piles. They would be covered in algae and filled with sickly fish... still alive, but sickly. I'd have an epiphany, "Oh right, I have fish!" then feel so bad that I had completely forgotten all about them for years. They hadn't been fed or care for in any way whatsoever.

Then I would realize that the fish had grown in numbers. Despite their lack of care, they had babies and were still alive even though they weren't healthy. I had this dream so often. Not always the same fish and not always in the same place, but they were there and it often followed this same pattern of being neglected, yet would still have survived. Not only that but they also reproduced. After quite a few of these dreams I began to question what they meant.

I had grown stagnant in my life. I forgot all about myself and my potential and all that I am. I neglected myself to where my spirit was sickly, yet my spirit still grew, it still survived, it even produced more. Those fish were me. My soul. My spirit. My potential. I had given up on myself, yet inside there was still hope. It was just waiting for the day when I would discover myself again... waiting to remember myself so that I could come back and grow and thrive and help others to do so as well.

In the dreams, when I would find these fish, I would immediately get them cleaned up and fed and taken care of. Despite my lack of care for them for years, underneath all of the clutter, they were there growing and readying themselves for the day they would be found.

They weren't the same as they were before they'd been forgotten. The years had changed them. They had adapted to their environment and even though it wasn't a healthy one, they were still doing the best they could and getting better than they were before.

Once they were all cleaned up and taken care of, they were stronger than ever and on top of that, they and their offspring knew that whatever happened in life, they now have the tools and knowledge to deal with it and continue to grow despite their surroundings.

After I had left my husband and was getting to know myself again, I once again dreamt of a fish. It was a beautiful shimmering gold Koi the size of a swimming pool and it was in a pool barely bigger than itself contained inside a room in a house. It made me excited to see it, yet at the same time I didn't know what to do with it. I remember asking for help.

Just this moment, I believe that fish, that enormous beautiful Koi, represents what I have to share with the world. It represents everything inside of me that is so big that it cannot be contained and must be shared. Perhaps one of its scales is this book.

IN CONCLUSION

I'm not saying that it is going to be easy... but what I am saying is that it is possible. There are people who have overcome huge afflictions in the world. They have moved on past added challenges to do amazing things that at one time, they and everyone who knew them never would have imagined they could do.

Imagining is a key part of the process. We've got to first imagine that we can succeed before we even look at solutions. If you didn't believe you have it in you to change, you wouldn't be reading this. We can learn this, even though we may have more challenges to overcome than most to get to the place most people are.

We imagine, we believe, we learn, we reflect, we do, we do some more... we continue doing through all the setbacks and backslides. We go back and imagine and believe and learn and do more again... we overcome, and we succeed.

Remember that every step is also a success. Every step is something that is overcome. Every time you have accomplished any part of this process it is a success. No matter which stage you are in, if you keep coming back, you have succeeded. There is no failure outside of quitting, and even quitting can be temporary. The first step is giving yourself a chance. Congratulations on taking that first step.

What steps have you taken that you can you congratulate yourself on?

Part IV

DO

Chapter 23

THE TRANSFORMATION

The following exercises are meant to help you on your journey. You don't have to do them all or exactly as I have them written. They are meant to be a guide. You can modify them to better suit you or just use them as is. You can also complete them in whatever order you choose. The order I have them in follows the order of the book... though there is no set order. It's like a dance. Maybe you'll do the two step, or perhaps you prefer a waltz or like my oldest daughter Selah who freestyles. Maybe you'll do all of the above.

There is not a straight and narrow exact path to perfection. That one led to where you are now. You'll go between all steps, back and forth, and all at once. This is your path. This is your journey. Enjoy it.

Look into your habits and your past. When you think back to your childhood, what were you like? Did you make decisions easily? Did you clean up after yourself?

_____
_____
_____
_____
_____
_____
_____
_____

What were your parents like? Did they expect perfection? Did they clean up after you? Were they messy? Were they spotless?

_____
_____
_____
_____
_____
_____
_____
_____
_____
_____

How about your teachers? Do you remember fights about cleaning or about stuff? About buying too much? Did you have too little?

_____
_____
_____
_____
_____
_____
_____
_____
_____
_____
_____

Really explore this and ask yourself even more questions that lead to a greater understanding of your past and the habits that have developed over time.

___

What keeps you from cleaning up your act?

___

Which of the physical challenges do you have in your home that makes it difficult for you to clean up?

_____
_____
_____
_____
_____
_____
_____
_____
_____

Which of the emotional challenges come into play?

_____
_____
_____
_____
_____
_____
_____
_____
_____
_____
_____

What solutions do you see that could apply to your life?

_____
_____
_____
_____
_____
_____
_____
_____
_____
_____
_____
_____
_____
_____

How do you distract yourself?

_____
_____
_____
_____
_____
_____
_____
_____
_____
_____

Are there other aspects in your life that I have not covered? Write it all down or just answer in your mind.

___

When you look around your home, what causes you the most grief?

___

What are the steps you would need to fix that one area? Write them down, step by step, so you can easily follow it. If you aren't sure, start with one of my suggestions in later pages.

_____
_____
_____
_____
_____
_____
_____
_____

Where do you currently sleep? Is that where you would like to sleep in your dream situation? Take time to visualize the bedroom you have now... only made beautiful and clean and styled in a way that brings you peace.... a way that makes it your own. Write down what you see.

_____
_____
_____
_____
_____
_____
_____
_____

Use these questions to spur you on to a more in-depth look into what is keeping you where you are, and what you can now do to make changes to those areas that hold you back so you can go forward. Look at which solutions apply to you and put them into action. Write down the action steps you will commit to taking.

VISUALIZE

Take some time to imagine what your home will look like all cleaned up. Imagine what your life will be like and how much easier everything will be when all that you own has a designated spot and all surfaces are clean.

Visualize how easy it will be to create a meal... from the time you come home with all of the ingredients that you need (not doubles of what you already have at home) using all of the tools you need to cook it, then to preparing it on your clean counters.

You have a sink full of hot soapy water so the dishes you dirty while preparing the food can be washed instantly and so that when you sit down to eat, the kitchen is already cleaned.

- Who would you have over for a visit? What would you do together?

_____
_____
_____
_____

- What hobbies could you now take up? What would you spend your time on now? Have you ever dreamed of creating art, or learning to play an instrument, or writing a book?

_____
_____
_____
_____

- Have you dreamed of having friends over to visit and even stay the night in your guest room or on the couch? How does that make you feel?

_____
_____
_____
_____

- What about simpler things? How would it feel to walk across your house without tripping on anything? What if you could do that in the dark in the middle of the night... without once stubbing your toes or stepping on something?

_____
_____
_____
_____

- How will it feel to wake up in the morning and know exactly where your keys are?

_____
_____
_____
_____

- To know what you have for food and what you'll need at the store.

_____
_____
_____
_____

- How does it feel to climb in to a freshly made bed with clean sheets straight from the dryer? To wake up and have every outfit you own cleaned and loved.

_____
_____
_____

- To have time to plant and tend to a vegetable garden.

_____
_____
_____

- To fit your car in the garage in the middle of winter.

_____
_____
_____

- To know exactly where your tax receipts are in tax season because you keep them all in one place.

_____
_____
_____

- To find the book you have been wanting to read and to be able to sit down in the clean living room to relax and read it.

_____
_____
_____

Imagine exactly what you would like your life to be like and what your home looks like when it is all clean. Imagine exactly how that makes you feel. Write out everything you visualized and how you felt. Transfer your most important and impactful visualizations to the lines below.

Schedule a minimum of 5 minutes right before bed to visualize just what you want your home and life to be like. Feel the emotions that come up in that dream life.

Spend a minimum of 2 minutes each morning visualizing your dream life as well and then take a few more minutes to write down your intention for the day to bring you closer to that dream.

Now write out two action steps that you will take that day that will bring you closer to your dream and follows your intention. Make that action step something you can stick to. It does not have to be big... it can be as simple as making your bed that morning. In the back of the book there is a template to follow. Feel free to make copies for your daily use. There will also be tools you can print out from the website found on our Facebook page.

20+ ACTION STEPS TO CREATE A BEAUTIFUL BEDROOM ENVIRONMENT

1. Open a window to let in some fresh air. If it is winter and it's cold outside, even a small crack will do.

2. Put on some inspiring music like the playlist at the back, or make your own.

3. Take everything off of your bed and make your bed. If the sheets aren't clean, strip the bed of its sheets and throw them in the washer while you work on the rest. Quickly make the bed with fresh clean sheets or if there aren't any, a blanket or two that you have and set the pillows out nicely. Don't spend much time on this because you'll be remaking it once the sheets are clean. There will be some back and forth until you have a system and the rest of the house is in better shape.

4. Pull everything out from under your bed so that it's completely clear and you don't miss anything.

5. For your initial cleaning, gather all of your clothes, both clean and dirty from all areas... laundry baskets, closets, drawers, floor, etc. After you've done this once, you keep clean and dirty clothes separate. If you know the clothes you have don't fit into your drawers and closet, take all of your clothes and put them on your made bed in like piles (pants, jeans, dresses, skirts, shirts, underwear, shorts, sweaters, and socks). Pick out your favourite top 10 from each pile that fit you. Pretend you are out shopping and are starting from scratch and you only have enough money to purchase ten items from each pile. Pick those ten. Once you've done so, throw them in the laundry hamper to be cleaned if you aren't already. If clean, hang them up or put them into your drawers. If you wouldn't buy ten in the store of the clothes you currently have, don't keep them just to make up the ten. If you wouldn't buy them

today in the store as they are... there is no sense keeping them.

6. If the clothes you've kept aren't clean, put them into the washer to clean while you work on the rest (if your sheets are still in there, put your favourite clothes in a laundry basket to go in next). Your basket should be emptied from Step 5.

7. If you are happy with the clothes you've kept, put the rest into a garbage bag and place outside of your house to bring to the second hand store or the garbage dump. If you have more room in your drawers and closet, and you wish to have more clothes than the 10 from each type, pick out the next top 10. If you just aren't ready to get rid of the excess, package it up so it is at least outside of your bedroom, and place in storage if you have the room. The point is to make your bedroom a nice environment so that you can get used to having a space that is clean and healthy and it starts to seep into your consciousness to become what you naturally want.

8. The sheets are probably now washed so put them into the dryer with a nice smelling dryer sheet if you use them. Skip this step if your sheets were already cleaned.

9. Do another load of laundry from all of the dirty favourite clothes that you have kept.

10. Grab a garbage bag. Set a ten minute timer so you speed through this step and don't over-think it. Throw all of the obvious garbage into the bag. If necessary, revisit this step once you get to the end.

11. Take everything out of your room that does not belong there. This step may take a while and may need to be broken down into smaller steps.

12. Designate a space for everything that you are keeping in your bedroom. If it doesn't fit, decide what gets to stay and what has to leave whether that means you get rid of it entirely (give it away or throw it away) or that it finds another place in your home.

13. Put everything away in its designated spot. If it doesn't all fit neatly, decide what goes. Your bedroom is going to be the one space you keep nice no matter what, and if it gets messy again, when you notice it's happening, schedule a time when you clean it again.

14. Your sheets may be dry at this stage. If so, go grab them and make the bed again using the nice cleaned sheets. Skip this step if your sheets were already cleaned.

15. Move the clothes from the washer into the dryer and put another load into the wash if there are more dirty clothes.

16. Get a bucket of hot soapy water to clean all non-fabric surfaces. If you don't have a cleaning bucket don't wait until you buy one, use an old ice cream bucket or even a sink. Use what you have that works. If you must, buy a bucket, keep it under the sink so that you will know where it is next time you need it. Use a soap that you love the smell of if you have it. Use what you have if you don't, or buy one nice small bottle of soap that you love the smell of.

17. Wash down all dressers, bed frame, and any furniture that is staying.

18. If the cleaning water gets dirty, dump it in the toilet (making sure everything in it can be flushed) and get new clean soap and hot water cool enough to have your hand in.

19. Spot wash any dirty spots on the walls.

20. Pick everything up off the floor and put away, throw away, or set in a box outside of your bedroom if it no longer belongs there.

21. Vacuum the floor if carpet. Sweep and wash the floor if not carpet.

22. To wash the floor, you can use hot soapy water and a clean rag or an old clean towel ripped into one to two foot squares. Wet your cloth in the hot soapy water and ring out most of the water so it doesn't drip but is still wet. Use elbow grease (your hard work) and scrub away at the floor until it's clean.

    Again, when the water gets dirty, get new water. Alternatively, if your floors are really bad you can use the water as it is until all the floor is done, then go and get new water and start over again. It may take many steps. You can follow this up with a dry rag to dry the floor.

23. Get the clothes from the dryer and fold them or hang them up and set in their designated spots.

24. Celebrate your nice clean bedroom in a way that makes you happy and keeps the room clean. It's probably late at night so maybe you can celebrate by climbing into those nice fresh clean sheets with a great book and read before bed.

25. In the morning when you wake up, take a nice big deep breath, look around your room and smile. Then turn around and make your bed again. It shouldn't take more than 2 minutes. Pick up any mess that may have happened from old habits, like clothes on the floor and that book you had from last night.

26. Think of ways to make it extra special in your bedroom such as using a nice natural air freshener like a diffuser and essential oils. Put up curtains that you like. Pick your favourite blanket to make your bed with. Set a nice vase of flowers that you will throw out when the flowers start to wilt and you'll change the water in every day.

I want you to start developing habits of keeping a nice space... it can start with your bedroom. I also want you to get a taste for what it is like to live in a beautiful environment. You deserve it. If that last sentence bothered you, I want you to start doing this next exercise diligently.

LOVE YOURSELF

Every morning after you wake up and make your bed, go to a mirror and look into your eyes. Tell yourself, "I love you" and use your name, and then, "You deserve a healthy life and a healthy beautiful environment. You are worth it."

I also want you to say those same words before bed. Do this every day and night until you start to believe it, and then keep doing it.

STEPS TO GETTING THE REST OF THE HOUSE CLEAN

Kitchen Dishes

1. If you have a dishwasher, fill it up in a way that the dishes get cleaned. Start with the dirty dishes where food isn't dried on and that can still get cleaned in the dishwasher.

2. If you don't have a dishwasher, pile like things together for washing... all plates in a pile or a few piles, all bowls / pots and pans nested together. Place all the silverware in a glass or big bowl together. This will make room to the right of the sinks, and then set a clean towel on the washed empty countertop for the clean dishes to dry on.

3. If the dishes are all really dirty then take a scrubby or scouring pad to use on a first round through the hot soapy water because you'll need to wash them twice.

4. Clean out both sinks and wash them. Fill one of them with hot soapy water. Put some of the glassware in that isn't really dirty so that the water stays clean longer. Wash the cleanest of the dirty cups and mugs. Rinse with clean water and set on a towel to dry.

5. Wash in order of glasses, mugs, silverware, plates, bowls, then pots and pans, large bowls, and anything else that is left. Alternatively to washing in the above order, you can start with the largest of dishes whether pots and pans or not, so that once clean, it makes room for all the rest. If you have lots of large dishes and cookware, this may be the way to go so that you create space right away.

6. Put all of the clean dried dishes away neatly in the cupboard where they belong. If they are still wet, use a clean dish towel to dry before you put them in the cupboard. Set them up in a way that makes sense to you. Where do you automatically go to open a door to find a cup? Set the cups in that cupboard.

7. When the water gets dirty, start bringing things through in order of cleanest to dirtiest and scrub off all the tough spots and put them into the second sink if you have one. If not, don't put them on the clean dishes, but set them apart from the dirty. Do this either until you've gone through all of the dishes or until the water is too bad to continue. These dishes scrubbed off in dirty water will need to be washed again.

8. Drain and fill again with fresh new hot soapy water and put the cleanest of the dishes you scrubbed in the water to clean. Only have enough to have some to soak while allowing you room to wash individually under the water.

9. If you run out of time before completing all of the dishes, make sure the dishes that got washed get rinsed right away and then dried and put away. You can drip dry them but if you are out of time, use a clean dish towel to dry them and put them away. You can also add a quarter cup of bleach to the hot rinse water as an added step to cleaning the dishes.

10. Drain the sinks and clean them up. Keep them empty and clean so that they are usable during the day when you aren't doing dishes. The countertop to the right should now also be empty so you can use that space to prepare food. Make sure to clean up the space again once you've made your food so it stays ready for you.

11. Get back to the dishes later today or set aside time tomorrow so that you get ahead on them daily until they are all done. Once they are all done, create a daily dish washing schedule to stick to.
12. Celebrate your progress!

Everything Else in the Kitchen

1. Once the above steps have been completed, move on to everything else in the kitchen. This can also be done before all of the dishes are cleaned just so that the rest of the room feels clean and you can prepare food safely and easily.
2. Pick up all garbage and put into the garbage can. Once full, set outside at the trash area and replace the garbage bag.
3. Clear off all countertops. If this is not possible due to more dirty dishes than you've had time to clean for the day, put all dirty dishes that are remaining to the left of the sink. If they don't all fit, get a box to set the rest in and set aside somewhere safe and close so you can get to them as soon as possible.
4. Wash down all cleared countertops with hot soapy water.
5. Pick everything up off of the floor that doesn't belong there so you can sweep. If there is still too much stuff in the kitchen because you have not gone through what is left yet, start by clearing floor space in front of the sink, stove, fridge, and dishwasher so that you can make progress. Each day you will want these cleared spaces to grow.
6. Wash the floor spaces that have been cleared with a bucket of hot soapy water. Change the water as necessary. It should feel clean to put your hands into with the rag. Rinse the rag in the bucket as it gets dirty.

7. Each day, grow your cleared spaces and wash more.

8. There will be more steps to add, the cleaner you get (such as washing cupboards inside and out, washing windows and clearing out the fridge and washing it out on an as needed basis)... these will also take less time the cleaner you get. Don't overwhelm yourself. Take time to breathe and appreciate each step you are completing.

9. Celebrate your progress!

Laundry

1. When you have piles and piles of dirty laundry, you may tackle this differently than when you are all caught up.

2. Gather all of the dirty laundry and put in one place in front of the washer.

3. Pull towels out of the pile and start up a load with those. Don't overfill the washer with towels but put enough in to make a good sized load. If you are unsure what that looks like, and you have your washer instruction book available, it should say in there how much you can put in. If not, look on YouTube or do trial and error.

    It shouldn't be so full that you are stuffing things in and packing them down. They should be loose enough that you could pack more in. Resist the urge to stuff it as full as you can because they won't come clean if overstuffed.

    At the same time, you don't have to make really small loads so that you never get ahead on the laundry.

4. Put like things together. All of the sheets in one pile, all the blankets together, all of the kids clothes in their own piles, all of your own clothes in your pile.

If you have gone through all of the action steps to creating a beautiful bedroom then you have already thinned out your clothes and will have a smaller pile than the rest. I suggest getting your children to each to go through the same process you had for your clothes and get rid of the extras, or ones that have been outgrown, or that have big stains or rips in them. Thin out all of the clothes and linens that are left so that you don't have to clean things you'll be getting rid of. Each person can be responsible for their own piles.

5. Keep the laundry going through the steps until all are done and put away... cycle them through the washer and dryer to folding and putting them away or hanging them up.

6. If you run out of time before you are done, then finish all of the steps for the last load that went into the washer and don't start another load until you are available to put them through all the steps to completion.

7. When all of the laundry is done, then you can create a system and pay more attention to putting whites with whites, jeans with jeans, colours with like colours, darks with darks and towels with other towels. Until then, just work on getting everything washed.

This is up to you to use whichever method you'd like. You will still want to avoid putting white clothes in with new coloured clothes or bright clothes that may bleed or they may end up pink or blue when you don't want that.

8. Set time aside each day to put at least one load through from start to finish.

Bathroom

1. Start with picking up all garbage into the garbage can and emptying that into the larger household garbage can.
2. Pick up all clothes and towels from the floor and put in the laundry hamper or in front of the washer if at that stage.
3. Put all of the stuff on countertop away neatly in drawers or outside of the bathroom where they belong.
4. Take anything left that does not belong in the bathroom out of the bathroom to where they belong. If not, put them aside to deal with later, but make sure they are outside of the bathroom.
5. Put anything remaining away.
6. Sweep the floor.
7. Use window cleaner or water and vinegar to clean the mirror.
8. Get a bucket of hot soapy water. Wash the sink and countertop.
9. If really dirty, use something like Ajax or even baking soda to loosen the grime.
10. Wash down the cabinets.
11. Tidy the bath and then use Comet, Ajax, baking soda or cleaner of your choice on the bathtub to get the grime off by sprinkling it around and then using your rag dipped in hot soapy water to scrub the tub and surroundings. Once cleaned, use just hot soapy water to rinse all the scrubby things off.
12. Wash the floor with hot soapy water.

13. Wash the toilet from the outside in. Start with back and wash the whole outside from the cleanest part to the dirtiest part.

14. Spray the inside of the bowl with cleaner and let sit. Use bowl cleaner instead if desired. Let sit for suggested amount of time and then flush or scrub and flush. Set out clean folded towels for your shower or bath time.

15. Celebrate! Be proud of yourself for all that you have accomplished.

GENERAL AND MISCELLANEOUS

Garbage

1. Make sure all garbage gets put into garbage cans.
2. Empty all garbage cans daily by putting all the filled bags outside in a garbage canister with a lid where it isn't an eyesore... where your pets or stray animals won't raid it.
3. Take the garbage to the curb to be picked up on garbage day if you have one. Set somewhere else neatly if you don't.
4. You guessed it... Celebrate!!!

Household

Create a daily, weekly, and monthly schedule for the following chores as well as any others that you may have.

1. Vacuum
2. Dust
3. Wash floors
4. Clean out and wash the fridge

5. Organize cupboards
6. Wash windows
7. Wash walls
8. Mow lawn
9. Create maintenance schedules for around the house and outside
10. Organize and clean the garage (this will have more steps involved and by now you can create a list that will help you)
11. Anything else I may have missed
12. Follow your list!

CREATING SPACE

After you've been taking care of your bedroom for awhile and the dishes have been getting cleaned and the laundry is in a routine, you will find you are ready to move on to other areas.

1. Rather than thinking of what you are getting rid of, think of it as creating more space. This is your most valuable possession of all outside of family (pets included) if they can be defined as possessions.
2. Set aside some time to work in a part of the house that is overcrowded. An area where there is a lack of space.
3. Go through a section of things that is taking that space from you. When you are ready, begin to give those things new homes... whether that be inside your house in its own space, or in another person's home, second hand store... or perhaps it's lived out its usefulness and it is time for it to retire to the garbage.

It's alright if this happens. It still exists in the world but is now being useful in another way... possibly even changing it into something else in the case of recycling. Wherever it is, it is not holding you hostage any longer.

4. This may take you the most time of all but needs the least explanation of how to do it because it is all in the mindset. This book will have helped you to see things in a new way. When you begin this journey with a clean bedroom, and keep on top of that one area, it will start to transform you from the inside out. The rest will come.

ANOTHER EXAMPLE OF A MORNING ROUTINE

1. Wake up to your clean bedroom.
2. Pick two things to be thankful for today.
3. Make your bed.
4. Spend at least 2 minutes visualizing your dream life. Eventually work your way up to 5 minutes minimum.
5. Write down your intention for the day. What is an outcome you would like to see from the day?
6. Write out two action steps that you commit to completing that day. Make sure they are something you can do for sure and don't rely on someone else to complete. Something that will bring you closer to your goal and goes along with your intention for the day.
7. Look yourself in the mirror and tell yourself "I love you" using your name, then, "you deserve a healthy life and a healthy beautiful environment. You are worth it."

8. Make the decision daily to change and do whatever it takes to get there.
9. Stand for a full minute in a power pose to increase your confidence in yourself. Think of wonder-woman with her hands on her hips, legs at shoulder width apart or of the marathon runner who just came in first place who stands with arms outstretched and head to the sky. These have been proven to build feelings of confidence. While doing the power pose, take deep healing breaths and count them. Notice how good that feels.
10. Say your affirmations while in power pose.
11. Take on the day with excitement and great expectations for your future and present.
12. Enjoy it!

You can also create your own magical morning routine. Imagine your dream morning and then write it out. Take steps towards creating it for yourself.

Pick one thing you can now incorporate into your morning. Be consistent with it. If it isn't how you do things now, it may take many attempts to have it come naturally without effort.

At the start it will require conscious intention to follow daily and you may not even be able to follow all steps as it is written down. You can make adjustments or look at why you weren't able to follow it. Make changes to set yourself up to succeed at it.

If your morning starts early, are you getting to bed early enough? You may need to pick one thing from your new morning routine and stick with it, making sure you do at least that one thing.

Start with making your bed as soon as you wake up and tidy your room. That way your bedroom stays clean. It only takes about 2-3 minutes when you start with a mostly clean room.

Once that has become habit and you do it without thinking, you can add another point from your dream morning routine. Continue that until you are living your dream morning every morning. Make adjustments as you wish.

When, or if, you find you've slipped back into old habits, acknowledge it, recommit, and get right back into doing what had been working for you. Don't beat yourself up about it. Just know that you aren't that old person any longer and aren't going to continue living that way.

Then decide who you want to be, and begin to live as that person... the new you with new values, new confidence, and new habits. They will come when you make the conscious effort to incorporate them daily.

My Example: March 2, 2016 Morning routine 5 and 6.

My intentions for today are to live as close to my dream visualization as possible, to face today looking at things positively and being aware of the possibilities. An outcome I would like to see are smiles on my children's faces tonight around the dinner table when we sit down to eat a healthy delicious meal that we all helped to create and laughter as we talk to each other and tell some of the great things that had happened today.

Two action steps I am committed to take today:

1. Go through all of the 20+ Steps to create a beautiful bedroom environment in my bedroom.
2. Go through all of the kitchen steps and add more to the book if I've missed anything. This is to set tonight's vision up for success.
3. I actually think that may be too many steps above because I have many steps within each step so I'd better revise so I will successfully complete them and feel good about having kept my word to myself. I can always do more once I have done what I committed to do.
4. Clean the dining room and set the table with a nice table cloth.
5. Take some boxes from my room and put them neatly into the garage, labelled.

ACCOUNTABILITY

1. Go online to the Facebook group "Careful Where You Set This Down" where you can have someone to check in with daily or weekly if you prefer or find a friend or family member willing to be your accountability partner.

    Ask if they will check in with you without any guilt attached. Only support. When you have moved forward from the last time they talked with you, celebrate together, with even something as simple as them telling you "well done! Great job." When you have slipped behind, they only help you discover what got in the way of your progress, not make you feel bad for it. Guilt just holds you back from progressing so you don't want more of that.

2. Commit to them and yourself one thing you will do before the next time you talk that will lead towards your progress. If that becomes simple and easy for you to do, add another commitment and action step to take.

3. If you cannot find someone supportive to help you, hire a coach to do the same. To find coaches specifically suited and trained in helping hoarders, join my secret Facebook group for more resources. If you do not want to confide in someone, I suggest doing what I started with. Write it in a journal. It's actually a good idea to keep a journal regardless of whether you find someone as an accountability partner/coach or not. Follow my lead and write out what worked and what didn't. Use this book, and once it's filled, start a separate journal. Revisit what you had written in this book and notice your progress in thinking patterns and actions taken. Write out your thoughts and your feelings while you are going through the process. You can do this in the same journal as your morning routine's intentions and action steps. It'll be good to keep it all in one place.

HELP! WE'VE LET THE HOUSE GET AWAY ON US

This is when you've fallen out of new routines and into old habits. The house is getting back to looking like a tornado, filled with messy mud pie making toddlers with clutter everywhere and you're getting overwhelmed again.

1. Pick a room to start in. Take a few deep breaths, close your eyes and visualize the room completely cleaned so you have a visual map to follow.

2. Turn some good energizing music on and crack a window open to let fresh air in

3. Sweep everything into a pile so that you get the maximum area cleared.

4. Pick anything you need or love (not to put more guilt on you but if you love it, treat it better than this), then wash it and put it back where it belongs.

5. Use a dustpan to gather everything else up and put into the garbage can. If it ended up on the floor, it isn't all that important and can go.

6. If you have time, wash the floors with a rag and a bucket of hot soapy water, or your preferred way of washing the floors.

7. Hot water should dry faster but if there are still wet spots when you're done, dry them with a dry rag.

8. Continue on with the regular steps from each section until you are back to a nice, clean, organized home.

Chapter 24
ADVANCED ADVICE

I thought we all could benefit by learning from people who naturally have an ability to keep their environment spotless most of the time and presentable all of the time. Somehow I have surrounded myself with friends who have always kept a clean home. They will share with you their secrets.

Heydi

"Everything in its place is important. I sometimes leave things out that need to go up or down the stairs but I give myself a routine as to when it will make it up or down and I don't leave it for longer than an hour usually, or at most, a day. If I haven't used it in a day it goes back where it belongs. That motivates me to do whatever I need to do.

Keeping my house clean, for me, is a respect thing for myself and my house. Whatever am I okay with total strangers seeing should be treated the same as what my friends see. Food wastage is punishable by not buying it again, or if half eaten and wasted a six month ban. It's the Catholic in me. Keeping my child clean and groomed is a simple self-sacrifice. This is my child. Am I parenting her at her best? I teach her self-respect.

What you said in your book about everything in its place is great. Everything in its place as quickly as possible and you can relax and not have to worry about anything that hasn't been done. The things that haven't been done have a timeline, therefore they do not cause stress."

Terri-Lynn

"I do it right away. I don't think about cleaning. The more I think about it, the more I will think about reasons or come up with excuses to put it off. I do it as soon as I can get it out of my way. I feel better and I stop a mess from accumulating.

I focus on one room at a time. It is easy to get distracted by a mess in another room while cleaning the first one. If distracted by one room it's easy to get distracted by others which can result in nothing fully clean and me fully unsatisfied. I complete one room first. Once I look around and see everything clean and tidy, it gives me more motivation to clean another room.

If the energy is there, I clean. I do it right away without stopping. I don't take breaks, I don't sit down and I don't put it off. If I feel that spurt of energy, I use it! I take advantage if I am feeling good and not feeling stiff to do the heavier stuff I'd normally put off like laundry and hauling the vacuum cleaner up and down the stairs. The easier lighter stuff can be done any time. Once I have things clean and tidy, I do touch ups once a week to avoid having to spend an entire weekend scrubbing my house because I put it off for so long. It is easier and faster to maintain a clean tidy home and keep my sanity and peace of mind if I don't have to think about the mess in my home on my way back from work after a long day."

Loretta (my mom)

I'll start off with something my mom wrote for and about me a few years back when she made the most beautiful photo albums for me. I'll then move on to what she wrote a few days ago when I had asked her to contribute to the book so people may learn from her.

I can see that in the photo album she looked at my traits from the positive aspect rather than from the perspective of frustration.

Around 2003

My daughter, Angel

"She is determined which can work to her advantage. She can be profoundly focused if she has a passion for something. She has a brilliant mind. She is a gifted character actress who struggles to find friends and lovers of good character (this has since changed for me on the friends' front so far). She looks only for the good in other people and often overlooks their flaws. She has a kind and loving spirit. With little effort she is beautiful, although this does not seem important to her. I love her big blue eyes, her perfect teeth and smile and I have always loved her chestnut hair. My fondest memories are of dressing her up and French-braiding her beautiful hair. Angel dearly loves her children and struggles to discipline them because she loves them so much. Despite that, her babies are beautiful spirited individuals and they always know the rules at Grandma's house.

What do I want for my daughter? I want her to be happy. I want her to follow her dreams. I want her to learn the value of common sense. I want her to learn to focus on things of importance even when there is no passion. There is joy in the completion of necessary tasks. I want her to take the time to enjoy her children today because tomorrow they will be grown up and have children of their own. I want her to find true love and friendship in people of good character. I want her to love God with all of her heart and with all of her soul and with all of her mind.

I am proud of you Angel, and I believe with all of my heart that you are capable of the dreams you have for yourself and of the hopes and dreams that I have for you."

March 2016

"I would never have thought that my daughter would one day become a hoarder. As a child she kept a messy room but no worse than any other child her age. She was sad when I would get rid of toys or clothes that she had outgrown but I didn't see that as an unusual response.

I remember the first time I noticed that something was wrong. I had gone to her small apartment to visit her and her new baby. I was speechless and horrified at the conditions they were living in. Since then over the years I have tried to help, cleaning with the kids when I was over to babysit, pushing all the clothes, toys, garbage into a pile in the middle of the floor, then enlisting the oldest granddaughter to help pick out what to keep, put away, wash or throw away. Washing peaking piles of crusty dirty dishes and pots. Throwing away dried up or rotten food in the fridge. Cleaning up spills long since hardened into a cemented mess.

It broke my heart and still does. There have been moments when I have given up on the entire situation but then I find myself hoping that maybe this time will be different. She will have found a way to keep her home clean and somewhat orderly. It does not have to be spotless but the chaos and disorder should not be the environment that my daughter and grandchildren live in. No one should live in an environment like that. It feels like there is a spiritual component to it, and not spirits of the Godly kind. Maybe this time will be different.

Angel asked me to put on paper some of the habits I use to keep my home clean. To start, I have a wonderful husband and we work together. We are not yet retired but we love our home and work together to keep it nice. Both of us work pretty much every day on our home. Some days we put in more time than others.

On rare occasions we don't do much depending on how we are feeling or how much sleep we got. I don't love doing housework, but I don't hate doing housework. I love to finish for the day and sit back in a clean environment, enjoy a tea and admire my beautiful home. I feel this way now and I felt this way when, as a young mother I lived in a tent, in an old log cabin, and in a very old 25 foot trailer with an electrical cord from the neighbours property to ours for power.

I do laundry almost on a daily basis. I don't like piles of smelly dirty clothes. I wash it, dry it, fold it, and then put it away. It's pretty easy these days with automatic washers and dryers. Not like using a wringer washing machine and hanging clothes on an outside clothes line. I try to iron my uniforms the day before I go back to work so I am all ready to go. I never leave washed clothes in the machine to mold and I never leave dried clothes sit in the dryer to become all wrinkled. So much easier to get it all done at once.

Dishes are washed every night to avoid getting all crusty and smelly. I have been tempted when we have had company for dinner. At midnight I would just like to go to bed and sleep, leaving the mess for morning. I just cannot do it even if it means another hour or two of cleaning. I'm so glad when I get up the next morning and my kitchen looks and smells beautiful.

Sometimes if there is lots to do and I'm feeling overwhelmed, I put my timer on for 30 minutes at a time and go from room to room getting as much done as I can in that 30 minutes, then add another 30 minutes to the timer. After a couple of hours it is amazing how much gets done if you are having a little race with yourself and your cleaning abilities just 30 minutes at a time. Other times I will stay in just one room until the time is up, then set the timer and go to another room.

Picking up, tidying and putting things away where they belong is done daily, sometimes twice a day. Dusting is done once a week when I am on my days off. Vacuuming is done daily because we have a dog that sheds. Bathrooms are cleaned once a week entirely; toilets, sinks, mirrors and floors. In between thorough cleanings, I use wet wipes to tidy up quickly, especially if company is coming. I try to wash the floors on my days off as well, so it gets done once a week. If I miss one week it's not a big deal to go two weeks if the floors are not too bad.

We make our bed every morning. I'd like to say I wash the sheets every week, but usually every second week. I keep only one set per bed, so as soon as they are washed and dried I put them on the bed. Saves having to fold fitted sheets!

Towards spring I start cleaning out my cupboards and drawers and dusting high shelves and cabinets that haven't been done for a year. Carpets get cleaned if needed with a steam cleaner. Once summer is here I spend all of my time outdoors in the yard in my flower beds. Then my house can get neglected as my yard becomes a priority. It never gets too bad, but that is why I do as much as I can before spring.

Anything that is broken or in need of repair is fixed right away. If things are left it won't take long for a home to fall apart. The garage and the yard also need to be cleaned and kept in order.

Once a year we go through boxes stored in the garage, throwing out or giving away things no longer needed or used. In some ways it seems silly to write things down or read another self-help book when you could just do what needs to be done. Work fast and get it all done. Don't piddle around and waste your time. Then you can have the pleasure of sitting down with a cup of tea and enjoy your beautiful home."

My Response: I just got back from mom's house. I'd gone to pick up the writing that she'd done for me. I thought I would add some of her traits. Even while visiting there today she does not sit still. She had a pot of homemade soup cooking on the stove for supper when I walked in, then made some bread in her new bread-maker, washed all dishes as they got dirtied in her hot soapy water in the sink and then got a rag out and began dusting all flat surfaces. She didn't stop. She didn't sit down. She kept working the whole time I was there because she was on one of her three days off per week.

That is the big trick. Just like getting in shape. For some reason I am always shocked when I hear from people who look naturally fit that they watch what they eat and they make sure to exercise at least 5 days a week.

My mom may "naturally" have a cleaned house but it isn't that way without action on her part. There is effort behind it and work behind it. There's a schedule and discipline involved. This may sound like a "duh" moment to some, but it was an epiphany to me. As mom told me today, it's hard staying fit but it's also hard staying fat, which one do you want to be? It's hard to get and stay successful, and it is hard to stay broke, so which will you choose? It's hard to keep a home clean and organized, but it is also hard to live in chaos and filth, which would you rather live in?

HELPFUL MUSIC PLAYLIST

- Arms of an Angel – Sarah McLachlan
- Let It Go – Frozen Soundtrack
- Another One Bites the Dust – Queen
- Give it Away – George Strait
- Give it Away Now – Red Hot Chili Peppers
- Brave – Sara Bareilles
- Go Your Own Way – Fleetwood Mac
- Happy Working Song – Enchanted
- Almost There – Princess and the Frog
- I Can See Clearly Now – Johnny Nash
- Freedom – George Michael
- Beautiful Day – U2
- Human Again – Beauty and the Beast Soundtrack
- It's a New Day – Will.I.Am
- Best Day of My Life – American Authors

DAILY INTENTIONS AND ACTION STEPS:

Today _____, my intention is:

_____
_____
_____

The goal I am working toward is:

_____
_____
_____

My two action steps I will take today to fulfill my intention are:

_____
_____
_____
_____
_____
_____
_____
_____
_____
_____
_____

Today _____, my intention is

_____
_____
_____
_____
_____
_____
_____
_____
_____
_____

My two action steps I will take today to fulfill my intention are:

_____
_____
_____
_____
_____
_____
_____
_____
_____
_____
_____

SPACE CREATION AFFIRMATIONS

- I get more and more organized day by day.
- Space is valuable. The more space I make in my home, the richer my life becomes.
- A space for everything and everything in its space.
- I complete my tasks from start to finish.
- My cupboards and dressers hold enough.
- I believe in myself. I can do this.
- I wash my dishes daily.
- I become free by letting go of stuff.
- I trust myself.
- I live with self-integrity and say no to what I don't want.
- My memories come from experiences, not from things.
- There is abundance in the world.
- Space is freeing.
- Better things are yet to come.
- I look forward to the future and enjoy my present.
- I love my life.
- I deserve to be healed.
- I deserve a clean environment.

www.ingramcontent.com/pod-product-compliance
Lightning Source LLC
Chambersburg PA
CBHW032108090426
42743CB00007B/285